CLEAN
BUSINESS
CUISINE
NOW
AND
Z/YEN

Milet Publishing Limited
PO Box 9916
London W14 OGS
England
Email: orders@milet.com
Website: www.milet.com

Clean Business Cuisine: Now and Z/Yen

First published in Great Britain by Milet Publishing Limited in 2000
Copyright © Michael Mainelli and Ian Harris 2000
www.zyen.com

ISBN 1 84059 227 3

Design: LOOK AT ME
Illustrations: James Verschoyle
Printed and bound in Belgium by Proost

CLEAN BUSINESS CUISINE

NOW AND Z/YEN

MICHAEL MAINELLI & IAN HARRIS

THIS BOOK IS DEDICATED TO OUR ANCESTORS,
FAMILY, FRIENDS AND COLLEAGUES, TOGETHER
WITH INFINITE GENERATIONS PAST, PRESENT
AND YET UNBORN.

P.S. DOES ANYBODY FEEL LEFT OUT?

CHAO KLI NING (499BC TO 401BC?): Quasi-mythological, proto-businessman from the late Zhou period in ancient China. Said to have had an uncanny knack for spotting an opportunity to make a quick buck. Legend has it that the Z/Yen business philosophy (see opposite), which later came to dominate the Early Imperial Eastern Mercantile Period, was founded as the result of a massive endowment from Chao Kli Ning's stupendous fortune (although some accounts attribute the Z/Yen Institution to Lo Fan, protégé of Chao Kli Ning, patriarch of the powerful Lo family and holder of Chao Kli Ning's subsidiary rights in perpetuity). The only evidence of Chao Kli Ning's existence is a rich oral tradition of case studies.

Z/YEN (PRONOUNCED "ZEE-YEN"): A mystical philosophy that encompasses enlightenment in business and enlightenment in life. Z/Yen is based on a unique blend of Taoism, Confucianism, Buddhism, decadent subcultures, arrogant supra-cultures and humour. The philosophy, which highlights the duality in all business problems and solutions, is sometimes summarised as "a philosophical desire to make money." Z/Yen is believed to have been founded by Chao Kli Ning (see opposite), although only fragmentary evidence of the origins of Z/Yen survives in its rich oral tradition. Historians have long sought documentary evidence of Chao Kli Ning, the origins of Z/Yen and the zest for enlightenment which made the ancient business world what it is today.

EXCERPTS FROM THE ENCYCLOPAEDIA OF BUSINESS ARCHAEOLOGY PRIOR TO THE DISCOVERY OF THE Z/YEN PAPERS – THE ANCIENT EASTERN BUSINESS TEXT CONTAINED HEREIN.

CONTENTS

EVERY DAY, IN EVERY WAY, THINGS GET BETTER AND WORSE

THE COLLECTED AFTER-DINNER REMARKS OF THE HOUSE OF Z/YEN

Z/YEN THINGS YOU ALWAYS WANTED TO KNOW ABOUT BUSINESS

In which characters from *The Z/Yen Papers* are introduced and the discerning reader can quickly surmise that one character, Chao Kli Ning, has an uncanny knack for making a quick buck.

WHILST MANY HAVE DEBATED the value of Z/Yen philosophy in business, even doubters often quote the following passage from the annals of Chao Kli Ning, or *The Z/Yen Papers*:

One day a strange runner came to Chao Kli Ning with ill tidings. He had run long and hard from Kli Ning's restaurant to Kli Ning's mansion. Thus spake the runner, "The enemy's army advances rapidly on full stomachs. Our army is lean and overly mean; it needs food. Hence our army has requisitioned all of your food and conscripted all of your restaurant staff, apart from me."

"One-legged Fong, I notice that these circumstances present you with the senior restaurant position. Give me a status report," requested Chao Kli Ning.

"The restaurant itself is intact, but the business is surely ruined," replied the winded runner, leaning heavily on his crutch.

"Get a big picture grip on the details, One-legged Fong. What about the customers,

environment, supplies, competition and cash position of my laundry?" enquired Chao Kli Ning.

"Sire, the laundry is not my responsibility. However, I could not help but notice that the laundry was inundated with customers. The laundry manager, Lo Fan, tried to conscript me himself. Several soldiers told me that they would have to wait days to have their uniforms cleaned. The town is a mess. And we have no restaurant staff. What do you wish me to do? Does Z/Yen show us the true way in such dire circumstances, or are we doomed to bankruptcy?"

"Z/Yen business philosophy is about total business improvement, not transient crises such as bankruptcy. You want easy answers, go read a book[1]. Now, please do excuse me. I must join my Z/Yen brothers who have gathered for our regular, midday commercial meditation."

One-legged Fong, knowing the power of Z/Yen and the wisdom of Kli Ning, patiently waited as the sun slowly moved west. Three hours later, Kli Ning emerged from the mansion. And he spoke, "One-legged Fong, listen closely. A well-fed man in a dirty shirt can clean his shirt. A hungry man in a clean shirt is still a hungry man."

Without further explanation, Kli Ning ordered One-legged Fong to buy all the ducks in the province, to buy all the rice the army had not seized and to buy all the tea a thousand men could drink in a year. Kli Ning also summoned Lo Fan and ordered him to

---

[1] It is unusual to the point of being strange that Chao Kli Ning uses the term "book" and not "scroll" in this encounter, but the ancient scrolls are unanimous and quite explicit.

purchase all the washing boards in the town, all the rope and twine the army had not seized and all the soap powder a thousand washers could use in a year.

One-legged Fong and Lo Fan exchanged glances, each wondering what on earth the old geezer was up to this time. Neither Lo Fan nor One-legged Fong were prepared for Kli Ning's next pronouncement. He ordered his calligraphers and messengers to post notices in all of the neighbouring villages and in all of the army tents: "Come to the Kwik Klining Duck Tea House and Laundry – all you can eat for a fixed price and get your laundry washed for free."

One-legged Fong and Lo Fan were astounded, but still unprepared for Kli Ning's final dictate. "Oh by the way, I know that you, Lo Fan, run my laundry and that you, One-legged Fong, run my restaurant. Well, it's time you both changed jobs. Take each other's. Lo Fan, you and your former laundry team shall become restaurateurs – playing host, preparing food, serving duck, rice and tea. One-legged Fong, you and your... well just you, you shall run a new laundry for all of my new clients."

One-legged Fong argued with Kli Ning, that without any staff, he would be unable to service so many clients. Kli Ning merely shrugged, "Get a detailed grip on the big picture, One-legged Fong. Run the laundry with all your heart and the staff will come." One-legged Fong bowed politely and withdrew, his heart full of despair. Lo Fan argued with Kli Ning, that he and his staff knew little about running a restaurant. Kli Ning merely shrugged, "Run the restaurant with all your heart and people will see the purity of your way." Lo Fan bowed politely and withdrew, his heart full of despair.

The calligraphers and messengers did their jobs too well. People came in droves to both the laundry and restaurant. One-legged Fong, unable to recruit a single member of staff and realising the wisdom of Kli Ning's statement, conceived a new way of laundering. The customers had to do their own laundry and eat their food while it dried, but they didn't mind. The washing boards, soap and water were cheap for a village which had none. As Kli Ning had predicted, the customers were prepared to be their own laundry staff. Lo Fan, unable to teach haute cuisine to a crew of scrubbers and realising the wisdom of Kli Ning's statement, conceived a new way of dining. He made it simple. The only offerings were duck, rice and tea. The portions were a standard size. The customers didn't mind. They could buy duck, rice and tea in a village which had none. Further, the restaurant was scrupulously clean. The tables were covered, for the first time, in crisp, white cloth. As Kli Ning had predicted, the customers saw the purity of Lo Fan's way.

Thus did Lo Fan and One-legged Fong achieve Z/Yen enlightenment. Thus did Kli Ning's turnover increase manyfold. And thus, as ever, did Chao Kli Ning enhance his fortune.

In our opinion, the case studies on the following pages, known colloquially as *The Z/Yen Papers,* represent a true and fair view of the account of Chao Kli Ning – restaurateur, launderer, Z/Yen business philosopher, and man with an uncanny knack for spotting an opportunity to make a quick buck.

- What could Chao Kli Ning have gained from significant hedging opportunities on ducks, rice and soap?

- Write an equal opportunities statement that would enable One-legged Fong to take Chao Kli Ning to arbitration successfully.

REMEMBER WHAT THE DORMOUSE SAID,
"FEED YOUR HEAD, WASH YOUR SOCKS,
DON'T EAT MY SHORTS"

LATE NIGHT RUMBLINGS OF THE KWIK KLINING DUCK TEA HOUSE AND LAUNDRY

WHAT IS THE SOUND OF AN
ARMY'S FOOTSTEP?

THE THOUGHTS OF CHAO KLI NING

CONFEDERAL UNITY

Wherein many pointless discoveries of great importance are made concerning the benefits of centralisation, and then successfully reversed.

IN THE BEGINNING THERE WAS CHAOS. This chaos may be called decentralisation. Chao Kli Ning looked down upon the chaos and thought it was inefficient. Moreover, it was adversely affecting his profit. He asked Lo Fan to summarise the underlying processes in his restaurant and laundry. Lo Fan replied, "People come in, we take their money, they go away." Kli Ning was enlightened and said, "You are quite right, Lo Fan, the common theme is soap and water. Henceforth we shall save both time and money. Take the clothes from this laundry and the dishes from that restaurant to the same place. There they shall be washed together to the benefit of our bottom line. And we shall name this place the Kwik Klining Duck Tea House and Laundry Sanitation Facility." Lo Fan saw the wisdom of this and replied, "O master, as you speak, so it shall be done."

And it was done. Many were the savings as Chao Kli Ning had foretold. Less soap was used. Fewer buckets of water were needed. Water heating costs

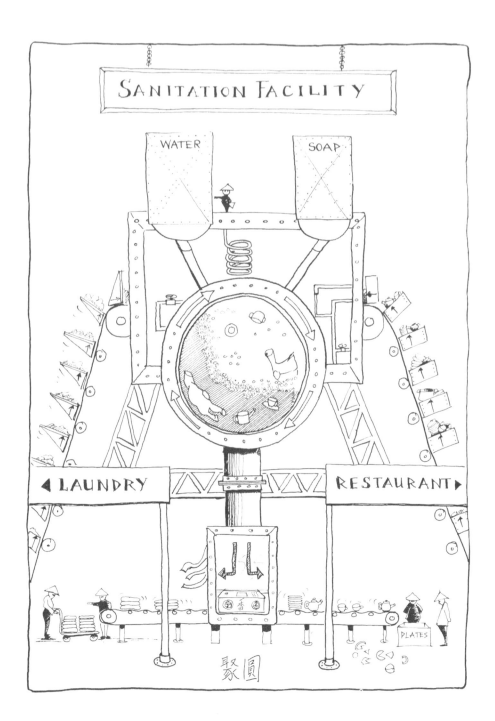

plummeted. Even Deng Zhou, the senior dishwasher, saw the benefits of change as his once onerous workload started to decrease.

There were a few wrinkles. Some laundry customers complained of unusual stains and a slight tea colour to their white garments. Others complained of missing small garments. The problem was usually temporary, as the restaurant manager almost always returned socks he found in the teapots. These complaints were trivial. Lo Fan confidently told the whinging customers that they could take their laundry elsewhere. He knew that this would have little effect on revenue. The nearest laundry was fifty leagues away. The dearth of alternative laundries was unsurprising. Chao Kli Ning's competitive business strategy included techniques that made the great general Sun Tzu a proud descendant of this progressive man.

Deng Zhou's ambitious niece, Yao Pi, had been a great help to Lo Fan in establishing the sanitation facility. As a junior dish washer, Yao Pi had been quick to adapt to the broader tasks of sanitation. She had identified many savings and had provided her uncle with perceptive career advice. Yao Pi was appointed head of sanitation. One of her first acts in this new role was to streamline decision making by appointing a deputy head of sanitation. Deng Zhou was encouraged to take early retirement. Yao Pi concentrated on reporting to Lo Fan and on a general sanitation strategy. Yao Pi ordered her deputy to liaise daily with the restaurant and laundry on demand and capacity.

Lo Fan saw many changes ahead and sought an audience with Chao Kli Ning. Lo Fan reported the changes already made and sought guidance on roles, responsibilities and general reporting structure. Lo Fan asked, "O master, is centralisation always better than decentralisation?" Chao Kli Ning replied, "Get a detailed grip on the big picture, Lo Fan. When should the caterpillar move his third leg?" Lo Fan pondered long and he pondered hard before he saw the wisdom of Chao Kli Ning's advice.

Sanitation collected and delivered dishes in batches three times a day. The restaurant manager, Po Chu, made some minor adjustments to restaurant operations to adapt to sanitation's routine. Firstly, he set aside an area for storing dirty dishes awaiting collection. He also instituted a standard form for tracking batches of dishes. He found it necessary to set aside an additional area for holding returned dishes prior to sorting and storing. Po Chu often found that there were few spare dishes ready for use. Following the fateful day when there were no teapots for six hours, he decided to place an order for additional dishes. He also hired a new dish manager to take responsibility for dish planning and supply.

The laundry manager, Wan Chang, made some minor adjustments to laundry operations to adapt to sanitation's routine. Firstly, he set aside an area for storing dirty laundry awaiting collection. Following customer complaints, including physical threats from village elders, he also established a small bleaching room for white garments. Many clothes in the large batches dried prior to ironing. Wan Chang installed a water tank for re-wetting these garments. He also hired a runner to retrieve stray socks from the restaurant.

One day Lo Fan was troubled. The bottom line had been getting worse. Lo Fan met with the laundry and restaurant managers. They both explained that there was less business in the cold winter months and that things would be better in spring. Lo Fan went to see Yao Pi, whose advice he valued. Yao Pi pointed out that costs were rising, particularly in the laundry and restaurant. Yao Pi suggested that management seek further efficiencies by centralising other processes, such as accounts. Lo Fan pondered long and he pondered hard on this suggestion.

Lo Fan went forth and sought an audience with Chao Kli Ning. Lo Fan brought grave news of worsening results, particularly with the extra staff, enlarged space and increased consumables. Chao Kli Ning was not pleased and vowed change. Chao Kli Ning asked Lo Fan to summarise his proposed solution.

Lo Fan replied, "Revenues down, costs up, save more money, centralise accounts." Kli Ning was struck with Z/Yen enlightenment and said, "Get a big picture grip on the details, Lo Fan. Each man should be responsible for his own destiny. Henceforth laundry and restaurant shall be rent in twain. Divide this sanitation facility. Thus laundry shall take unto laundry and restaurant unto restaurant. And we shall name this process the Kwik Klining Duck Tea House and Laundry In-Line Product Process Streaming." Lo Fan immediately saw the wisdom of this and replied, "O master, as you speak, so it shall be done."

And so were changes made. Many forms died that day. The customers found fewer socks in their teapots and a surprisingly white wash. The restaurant found it easy to return to old ways, with Yao Pi's former deputy as senior dishwasher. The laundry found that it could charge a premium for extra-white bleaching. Yao Pi eventually found re-employment as junior dishwasher at her uncle's retirement home.

■ Did centralisation work for the Kwik Klining Duck Tea House and Laundry?

■ Would Yao Pi's career have benefited from proper succession planning?

DECENTRALISATION IS ESPECIALLY
GOOD AS LONG AS EVERYONE MARCHES
TO THE SAME BEAT
(POSSIBLY FROM) FEAR AND LOATHING IN SHAANXI

THE RICHER THE BOY, THE BIGGER THE TOY
(EVIDENTLY FROM) CHAO KLI NING'S EVIDENT EXPENDITURE

GIZMO'S BIG ADVENTURE

Where Chao Kli Ning was overcome by gadgetry and may have missed a big opportunity to make a quick buck.

IT IS A TRUTH UNIVERSALLY ACKNOWLEDGED, that a single business in possession of a good fortune must be in want of some ultra-sophisticated apparatuses[2]. Chao Kli Ning's business, the Kwik Klining Duck Tea House and Laundry, was the big exception. Not for Kli Ning the come-and-go fashions of high technology that no one understood. Not for Kli Ning the passing fads of do-it-all machinery that constantly needed mending. Kli Ning was too hard-headed to be anything but practical, until the day he first saw the abacus at Sha Ky's rickshaw works.

Kli Ning was unsure what the abacus did, but he immediately saw its potential. As the senior executive of the Chao Kli Ning laundry and restaurant works, he could feel the intense power of Sha Ky's enormous central abacus room. The quiet hum of beads slithering up and down their appointed paths,

---

[2] In Sinkiang province "apparati" is the accepted plural of apparatus.

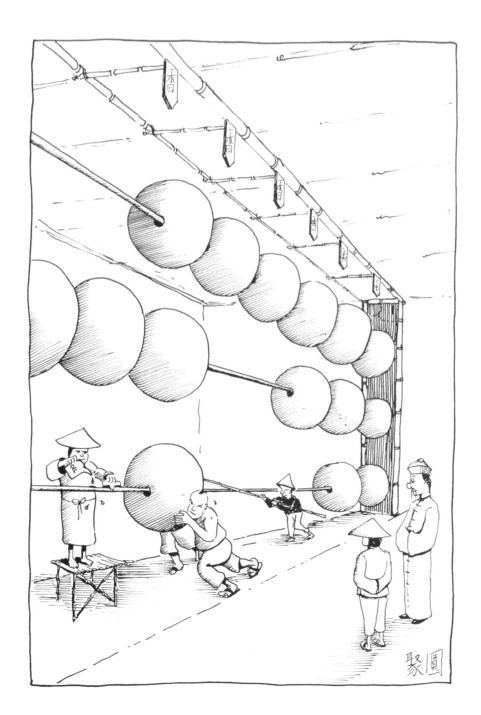

the fevered concentration of the abacus operatives as they oiled the rods, the mystical significance of the numerical workings – all these instilled in Kli Ning a vision for the future of laundry and restaurant administration. He could envision an abacus at every table, an abacus at every counter and a personal abacus for every employee regardless of age or status. Kli Ning wanted an abacus, and he wanted one badly.

"Let me get a detailed grip on the big picture. What does this abacus do, Sha Ky?" asked Kli Ning.

"You see before you the heart of our rickshaw operation. Without this abacus, we wouldn't know how much bamboo to order, we couldn't pay our employees, we wouldn't even know how many rickshaws we have in stock."

Kli Ning surveyed the five rickshaws in stock before noting, "Yes, I can see how frightfully complex this operation must be."

Sha Ky beckoned to Gi Zmo, her chief abacus controller and asked him to explain the fundamentals of abacus processing to Kli Ning. The explanation was abstruse, but Kli Ning grasped the basics with ease...

"...of course everything occurs here in base six. We have plans to double our capacity, but in this warehouse we can only store numbers less than 1,296 due to the weight of one kwong stone beads. If you notice the four men struggling with the ten kwong stone bead on the far side of the room, you'll get an idea of our other beadware constraint. As they push it up the rod, with the two boys oiling ahead of them, you can see that communication times, bead rates as we call them, would decrease if the temperature increased by much. At certain temperatures we find that the operatives' heat-stroke rate can crash the system."

It was at this point that Kli Ning began to take notes. Spurred on by Kli Ning's obvious enthusiasm, Gi Zmo's explanations became somewhat technical. Those details have been omitted from this text, as they would serve no useful purpose and may cause unnecessary anxiety to those readers of a slightly nervous disposition.

Kli Ning's abacus arrived three days later. The ABM (Abacus Business Machines) salesman assured Kli Ning that the 5691 Q series was a more advanced model than Sha Ky's, with enhanced rodware. Further, this model was specifically designed for the restaurant industry. ABM was so committed to supporting the restaurant industry that it was about to launch a new version of the abacus manual (readware) with improved table-counting functions. Kli Ning then knew he had bought the right machine.

Kli Ning explained the proposed operation of the machine to the head cashier, Qia Ming. Kli Ning described the wonderful new abacus room, where all information could be effortlessly produced with the push of a bead. The 5691 Q would change the whole way that Qia Ming and his staff worked. Qia Ming then knew that Kli Ning had bought the wrong machine.

Qia Ming had a subtle sense of humour. It was so subtle that there were no recorded cases of anyone detecting its existence. When Lo Fan, the restaurant manager, fell into the sanitation facility, Qia Ming merely tutted and said, "Kli Ning told us that this facility would clean up our staffing problems." Had Qia

Ming possessed a discernible sense of humour, it would have failed when Kli Ning poached Gi Zmo, Sha Ky's chief abacus controller, and sat him opposite Qia Ming in the cashier's office. Strangely, Sha Ky seemed unperturbed at losing Gi Zmo, and her wry remark, "Thank you very much," had a ring of sincerity rather than sarcasm.

Gi Zmo took control of the situation immediately. The primary function of the new machine was obvious. Tableware. Once all 65 tables had been counted, Gi Zmo thought long and hard to conceive a secondary function for the new machine. He started counting the beans – black, red, yellow, mung, aduki and soya – but couldn't keep up with the chefs. Gi Zmo tried placing the mung beans by the window and the aduki beans by the wall, but it was useless. Gi Zmo gave up bean counting. Nevertheless, the term bean counter has been retained in the annals of accountancy history.[3]

Eventually, Gi Zmo realised that the true benefit of the ABM 5691 Q in a restaurant environment must be the timely and precise computation of customer bills. He immediately set to work and developed a mechanism for bill production that would enable a trained professional to input, verify and output an accurate bill. He tested the mechanism thoroughly and presented his proposed changes to Kli Ning. Kli Ning was delighted and decreed that the ABM must be used henceforth for all bill production. Gi Zmo then moved on to bigger and more important business problems such as ensuring an even

---

[3] Even to this day, in Sinkiang province, mung means debit and aduki means credit.

number of chopsticks.

All of a sudden, Qia Ming was having problems with the bills. Firstly, only two waiters were capable of understanding automated bill production. These two staff then seemed to spend all their time doing bills. Secondly, the process took an extra ten minutes at the best of times but became interminable when the bead pushers took their tea break. Thirdly, customers didn't seem to understand the effort required to produce a bill and annoyingly requested extra drinks while they were waiting for their bills to arrive. Naturally, the whole bill production process then had to be repeated.

Qia Ming complained to Kli Ning about the extra work and the delays. Kli Ning was displeased and concerned. In his enthusiasm for the new machine he had already placed a large advertisement in the village gazette: "Come to Chao Kli Ning's Restaur-a-mat. See your bill computated mechanistically through the magic of a hugely expensive ABM 5691 Q series abacus." True, Kli Ning had managed to sting ABM to go halves with him on the advertising costs. Nevertheless, he had invested heavily in this venture and everyone had promised him that it would work perfectly.

Kli Ning demanded an explanation from Gi Zmo. Gi Zmo assured Kli Ning that he was ninety-five per cent of the way to speeding up bill production from ten to seven minutes; he just needed to finalise the change request form with Qia Ming and procure some new expensive rod oil greaseware. The greaseware would justify its vast cost by speeding up the bead rate quite a bit.

Qia Ming soon started to find his own solutions. He had hired two extra waiters to cover the ABM professionals' tables. Qia Ming had also succeeded in subtly dissuading customers from placing late orders for extra drinks. He achieved this by placing a large sign above the door which read: "Ordering drinks after calling for your bill is strictly forbidden."

When Kli Ning saw the sign, he was furious. He demanded an explanation from Qia Ming. Qia Ming assured Kli Ning that the sign worked in most instances. On the rare occasions that customers did not submit to the rule, Qia Ming could easily manage the situation by either giving them free drinks or banning them from the restaurant. In any case, the sign was only temporary, as Gi Zmo had assured both of them that he was ninety per cent sure that he was ninety-nine per cent finished with finding a solution. Within a week, all would be well, all being well.

Within a week, Kli Ning followed up on progress with Gi Zmo. Gi Zmo was optimistic. The solution was ninety per cent complete, and only a few minor problems remained. Gi Zmo was seventy per cent sure that there could be a suitable resolution to ninety per cent of the remaining problems if only Kli Ning would provide him with another ABM for development and testing. Kli Ning was one hundred per cent sure that Gi Zmo would advance his career more positively by seeking a challenging position elsewhere.

Kli Ning called Qia Ming before him and gave Qia Ming custody of the ABM contraption. Qia Ming expressed intense gratitude for the honour Kli Ning had bestowed upon him. Without questioning Kli Ning's eminent decision, Qia Ming merely said, "I can make it count to anything but it may add to nothing." Kli Ning tried to detect Qia Ming's subtle humour, and, in so doing, gained profound enlightenment into the Z/Yen of abacus maintenance, saying, "May you get a big picture grip on the details."

Kli Ning laughed as he threw out all the ABM equipment. Kli Ning laughed as he told Qia Ming to get rid of two waiters. Qia Ming failed to detect Kli Ning's subtle sense of humour but succeeded in firing the two ABM professional waiters. True, they were long-serving staff. True, they had once been popular with the customers and other waiters. Now, however, they just spoke abacus jargon. Bead rates, greaseware and the next generation of 5691 Qs soon bored their colleagues and the customers. No one regretted their departure. Naturally, they soon found lifetime tenures as professors of abacus science and fellows of the Institute of Abacus Professionals.

Some time later, Kli Ning encountered a strange monk begging for alms. This monk had a long beard and sandals, and muttered strange numerical incantations to himself, in particular the mantra "bead rate, base Tao." Kli Ning supposed that the monk was a Yen Buddhist, a more ancient sect than Zen. Yen Buddhists were dedicated to the pursuit of salvation, enlightenment, harmony, and hard currency beneath a stable exchange rate mechanism. As Kli Ning pondered the mantra, he then realised that this monk must be Gi Zmo.

"Bead rate, base Tao."

For the second time in his life, Kli Ning gave a small contribution to a begging monk in exchange for a brief conversation and some salvation for his conscience.

"Gi Zmo, hello, glad to see you looking so well," commented Kli Ning. "So, are you still into abacuses?"

"Bead rate, base Tao," replied Gi Zmo as he pulled a small personal abacus from beneath his robes and instantaneously clocked up the decimals required for Kli Ning's meagre donation.

"That little abacus is a fascinating device," said Kli Ning. "How does it work without a machine room and greaseware?"

Gi Zmo's eyes rolled before he replied, "Oh, this is nothing. The real future is digital binary. Bead rate, base two. That's a virtual certainty. I don't mean two fingered counting, I mean lots of ones and zeros everywhere. Binary is where the future's at. Yes it is, no it isn't. And artificial intelligence too, although I'm a bit fuzzy on that stuff."

Kli Ning persisted, "This micro-abacus, could I buy one?"

Gi Zmo responded, "As the sage says, 'A man with one abacus knows his sums; a man with two abaci is never sure'."

"Don't you mean two abacuses?"

"I'm not sure," replied Gi Zmo.[4]

Kli Ning was a little sad to see Gi Zmo in this muttering state. Kli Ning was a little happier when Gi Zmo wandered off and inflicted his mutterings elsewhere. Once he had recovered from the embarrassment of being seen with that lunatic monk, Kli Ning mused on Gi Zmo's ravings. Kli Ning applied his

---

[4] In Sinkiang province "abacuses" is the preferred plural of abacus.

vast knowledge of the world of business and exercised his uncanny knack for spotting an opportunity to make a quick buck, before deciding, "Digital binary, lots of ones and zeros, that couldn't possibly catch on."

QUESTIONS FOR STUDENTS

Would this tale have been significantly different if recounted in base three?

Reprogram the bootstrap for the ABM 5691 Q to enable laundry mungs and restaurant adukis (debits and credits).

THE OFF'S AND ON'S OF LIFE
ARE ALL BUT A SINGLE BITE OF
THE ETERNAL CHERRY

A BASIC TAO RESPONSE TO Z/YEN

THE TRULY SELFISH MAKE PEOPLE
HAPPY FOR THEIR OWN ENDS

(TRULY BELIEVED TO BE FROM) THE TRULY PROFOUND
THOUGHTS OF CHAO KLI NING

PEOPLE ARE FOR TURNING

In the course of which many character flaws are revealed under the stress of competition. Yet, as always, our heroes eventually emerge victorious, or at least profitable.

IT WAS THE BEST OF TIMES, it was the worst of times. Everyone was happy, everyone was sad. Not only that, everyone had a hangover. It had been a great New Year celebration. It had been a terrible year. It had been a pig of a year. This is the story of that terrible year.

It was the year of the Pig. Spring. The snow had melted. The birds were singing. The workers were busy. The competition was hotting up. Chao Kli Ning had his first meal in the village's newest restaurant. The new restaurant had received rave reviews. It was the "in" place for the "in" crowd. Very few civil servants could afford to eat there. Kli Ning cursed the new owner's name with every mouthful. This left a rather unsavoury mess around him. "Chung Chong Chop." At least, that's what it sounded like when Chao Kli Ning said it.

Chung Chong Chop had everything. He had inherited a small fortune, although it didn't look so small to Chao Kli Ning. With the fortune, Chung had acquired a winsome wife, Lin. And a dubious reputation for wooing

...WHEN TWO LOCAL DIGNITARIES SAID THEY WANTED TO SPLIT THE BILL...

beautiful mistresses. And he lived in a ravishing house. Kli Ning could cope with the thought of the wife and the dubious reputation, but the thought of the house gave him heartburn and the damage to Chao's own restaurant trade hurt his pride.

Chung Chong Chop had recruited most of Chao Kli Ning's staff. Chung paid the best wages in town. Kli Ning knew that Chung paid the best wages because Lo Fan, his restaurant manager, continually wanted to raise wages to keep Chao's staff. Since working for Chung, Kli Ning's former staff had all acquired absurd pretensions. In fact, in the service of Chung they had all acquired identical absurd pretensions. Character was contrary to Chung's restaurant policy. It wasn't just the wages, pretensions and conformity. Chung's staff also had exquisite uniforms. Kli Ning took pains to point out to Lo Fan that the uniforms were not pure silk, just a silk/cotton mixture. Lo Fan praised the leather shoes. Personally, Kli Ning preferred composite soles. Kli Ning also felt that if he had invented the sombrero, it would not look that way.

Lo Fan had his own problems with the Kwik Klining Duck Tea House and Laundry. Kli Ning's restaurant had lost all the best staff. Lo Fan had hired some temporary staff. Some of them didn't cut the mustard. Some of them couldn't chop ginger. One who could cut neither the mustard nor the ginger did try to cut the customers. He wielded a handy cleaver when two local dignitaries said they wanted to split the bill. No matter how shabbily dressed, both old and new staff demanded clothing allowances and persistently wanted to dress up in preposterous ethnic outfits. Further, Lo Fan had many sleepless nights after a particularly vivid nightmare in which each member of staff, accompanied by Lo Fan's wife Lo Tzu, all dressed in increasingly bizarre costumes, poured a vial of rat poison into the soup of the day (hot and sour with pork dumplings and a hint of ginger).

High on a mountain top in the groves of a secluded retirement home, a bleary-eyed Lo Fan sought counsel from the wisest source he knew. His mother listened carefully. Then, in the incessant, unbearably loquacious verbosity of the old, she asked the long-winded question, "Does the bullock change course when beaten?" As Lo Fan walked down the mountain he thought long and hard on his mother's question. He kicked a few sheep out of his path as he descended. Suddenly he recalled the ancient Way of the Stick at which his mother was so adept. His childhood training flooded back in an overwhelming rush. He remembered the arts in which he had been schooled – beating, flogging, cursing, kicking, blaming, and other such facilitation skills which guide subordinates towards the proper course of action. He resolved to follow the ancient Way of the Stick with gusto.

Lo Fan followed family tradition and installed himself as kitchen tyrant. The staff had never had it so bad. They could not stand the heat, so they got out of the kitchen. The staff fell over themselves in their desire to get out and serve the customers. Lo Fan was gaining a discerning clientele who appreciated good service and were rather impervious to bewildering fashion statements. Unfortunately, the head chef had enough of Lo Fan's author- itarianism and decided to get out of the kitchen permanently. No one gave

Kli Ning's restaurant good reviews any more. The restaurant then lost the discriminating clientele who recognise good food when they read about it. He also lost the few who recognise good food when they taste it. Lo Fan saw that things were going nowhere; Kli Ning despaired of ever again owning an impressive house. Chung noticed little except that some of his clandestine mistresses were now regularly seen wearing his staff sombreros around the village.

Kli Ning was not in a good mood. His wife, Cha, had spent a tidy sum on an absurd over-sized hat called a sombrero, while telling him that his restaurant seemed "so down market." Kli Ning demanded change from Lo Fan. The staff did not speak eloquently like Chung's staff. The costumes worn by Kli Ning's staff were uncoordinated and unacceptable. Lo Fan gathered quotes for elocution lessons and uniforms. Kli Ning demurred. He said, "Get a detailed grip on the big picture, Lo Fan. If you can't change the people, change the people," and went home. Lo Fan understood his master's proclamation, at once dismissed all the staff and advertised all positions through the village grapevine: "Staff wanted at Chao Kli Ning's. Long hours. Hard work. Adequate pay. No uniform."

As dusk fell, Lo Fan settled back in a chair in the quiet restaurant, with the satisfaction of a day's work well done. Kli Ning returned to a restaurant devoid of diners, and staff. He was outraged. Not only had Kli Ning spent most of the day widening his bedroom doorway to accommodate Cha's absurd sombreros, but then his restaurant manager had taken Kli Ning's suggestion to change the staff literally, when all that Kli Ning wanted was an inexpensive change management programme.

Doubting Lo Fan's ability to comprehend even the simplest Z/Yen proclamation, Kli Ning implored Lo Fan to seek the best counsel he could find. Lo Fan agreed. His mother had got him into this mess; she could get him out. Further, Lo Tzu was intractable these days. A trip to see his mother might remedy the situation. He would take Lo Tzu with him for a short sharp shock of maternal wisdom. The sombrero would stay at home.

Lo Fan's mother listened carefully to his latest woes. She reprimanded Lo Tzu for climbing the mountain without so much as a hat to protect her head from the sun. Turning to her son's need for counsel, she then, in the succinct way of the old, whose antiquity makes them sensitive to the value of time, laconically replied, "Son, get a big picture grip on the details. Do not fight with another's bow and arrow, do not discuss another's faults, do not interfere with another's work, do not beat another's bullock. And remember, you can achieve more with a trout than a stick."

As Lo Fan walked down the mountain he thought long and hard on his mother's suggestion. Surely she wasn't suggesting that he beat Lo Tzu with a trout? Suddenly he recalled the ancient Way of the Carrot at which his mother was not so adept (because she had a strange tendency to confuse vegetables with fish). His adolescent experiences flooded back in an overwhelming rush, in particular the manoeuvres he had learned to dodge low-flying halibut. He also remembered the arts which he had developed – leadership, self-improvement, building consensus, consultation and selflessness. Lo Fan resolved to follow the ancient Way of the Carrot with gusto. His resolve would be like a slap in the face with a wet fish to Lo Tzu.

Lo Fan re-advertised all staff positions through the village grapevine: "Staff wanted at Chao Kli Ning's. Reasonable hours. Moderate work. Good pay. Nice uniforms. Free elocution lessons." Lo Fan wisely visited the former head chef to plead personally for his return. Once he had been promised a special uniform the head chef returned. He was delighted with his ten-gallon wig. The rest of the staff soon followed. They were all delighted with their six-gallon wigs. They were pleased with their composite-sole shoes. Some found the all-cotton shirts hard to iron. Lo Tzu made a personal innovative fashion statement: an eight-gallon wig over a sombrero.

Some things were looking up. The staff were happier under the Way of the Carrot than they had been under the Way of the Stick. The good restaurant reviews returned. Income was rising. Some things were looking down. The composite soles on the staff's shoes started to come apart alarmingly quickly. Lo Fan was spending more money on uniforms than he thought possible. Customers observed that staff spent so much time preening themselves in front of the mirror that it was difficult to place an order. Other customers complained of wig hairs in their soup. In short, after all these changes, Kli Ning's restaurant was still nowhere near as profitable as Chung's. Chung noticed little, except that his clandestine mistresses were now regularly seen wearing wigs over his staff sombreros.

Kli Ning had had enough. He imparted some wisdom to Lo Fan. This wisdom had been handed down from generation to generation in Kli Ning's family. "Get a big picture grip on the details, Lo Fan. Generate some real profit in the next three days and you will be amply rewarded. Fail to do so and you will be fired. Thus do I meld the Way of the Carrot with the Way of the Stick. This is the Way of the Sticky Carrot." Lo Fan was astonished that Kli Ning had such insight into the ways of the retirement mountains, although Lo Fan recalled that this particular way was really named the Sticky Trout. Nevertheless they were both enlightened and knew how to proceed.

Lo Fan was indeed amply rewarded, well within the three-day deadline. A simple notice in Chung's kitchen did the job for Lo Fan. Once Chung's staff were aware of the significance of their wives' sombrero fad, it was only going to be a matter of time before Chung's popularity subsided. It was a matter of half an hour. The speed and efficiency of Chung's fall from grace shocked even Lo Fan. By nightfall, Chung sat in the village square, covered in plum sauce and duck feathers, cursing his libido. He now had no staff, an estranged wife and a pile of discarded hats. Only Lo Tzu, always a non-conformist, persisted with wearing the outmoded sombrero. After losing so much and gaining so little, Chung thought it best to leave town with Lo Tzu and inherit another fortune elsewhere. Chung graciously handed over his restaurant to Kli Ning with barely a spit or a curse. Kli Ning was ecstatic about his new restaurant. He noticed that his wife, Cha, stopped her mysterious crying after a few weeks. Lo Fan seemed strangely unperturbed at losing his wife to Chung. Indeed, he seemed in unusually high spirits and was often seen skipping, especially when he visited the grand house in which Chung Lin, Chung Chong Chop's estranged wife, still lived.

Having regained his monopoly of the village restaurant trade, Kli Ning prospered. He kept both restaurants largely unchanged in order to increase trade, although he insisted on composite soles for all uniforms. As an economy measure, he and Lo Fan combined the New Year celebration for the staff. Kli Ning named the celebration "Party on Chung". The staff were not happy. The staff were not sad. The staff were not mixing with each other. One side abhorred pretentious accents. The other side scoffed at cotton clothing. Kli Ning and Lo Fan schemed about the cost reductions they could achieve by putting all staff on equal and less extravagant benefit packages. Deep in his heart, Kli Ning knew that the more two sides compete with each other, the more they look like each other. He would have both groups of staff wearing the same uniforms before the end of spring. Spring came early that year.

■ Design a more appropriate uniform for an ancient restaurant taking due account of modern fashion, hygiene and safety regulations.

■ It was something Lo Fan said that caused his wife to leave him. Discuss at home.

WHEN THE TIGER FIGHTS THE
LION, THEY BOTH USE THEIR FANGS.
DOES THE HUNTER NOTICE THE
DIFFERENCE IN THEIR TEETH?

SUN TZU KNEW MY GRANDSON

IS IT BETTER TO TRAVEL
THAN TO ARRIVE?

THE ART OF WASH

QUALITY IS FREE

Whereby quality standards struggle to meet customers' innermost desires while removing foul smells.

ONE FINE DAY TAI TSO NOTICED a difference at Chao Kli Ning's laundry. That morning, as usual, he was the first villager to leave his washing. Tai Tso liked to get to work a little before everyone else. He worked at the village noodle factory, as the principal noodle inspector. His main concern was ensuring that noodles were cut to the right length. He appreciated the early mornings to himself, a small cup of tea, a chance to ponder on life's mysteries, some time to read the news. What was different about the laundry? It wasn't the stench in the air. The stench was always there.

Perhaps it was nothing special, but the laundry staff seemed more ardent. The counter woman nearly tore his laundry bundle from him in her enthusiasm to wash it. On his way home, Tai Tso took the time to quiz Lo Fan, the laundry manager. Lo Fan was delighted at Tai Tso's interest and said so.

"I am delighted," said Lo Fan. "What do you think seems different?"

"I don't know, a certain something. The look in the eyes. A smell of fear.

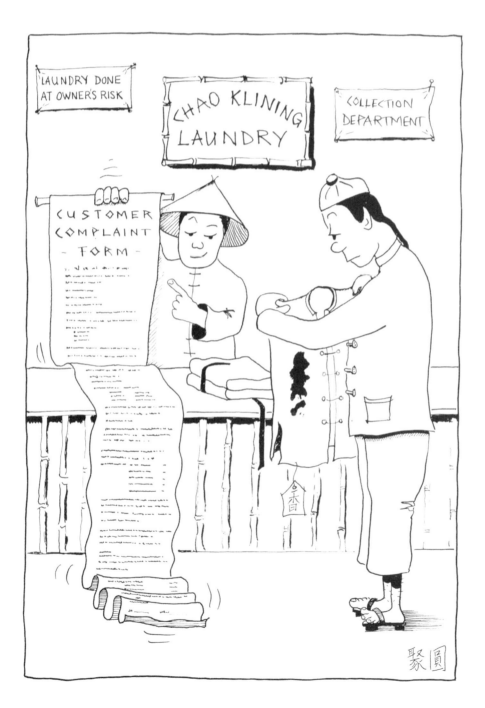

CHAPTER FOUR: QUALITY IS FREE   53

I don't know, just different. Come on Lo Fan, is something going on?"

Lo Fan replied proudly, "I didn't expect anyone to notice so quickly, but we have found a new way. The master from the Ganges, Guru Neverminda Widequal, has led the Kwik Klining Duck Tea House and Laundry away from the dualism of Confucianism and Taoism. Now we follow one pure path. The way of Ti Ku."

"What is this Ti Ku, Lo Fan? Is it one of these new ecological washing powders?"

"Certainly not," said Lo Fan, "it goes much deeper than that. Guru Neverminda is a very wise man. A very, very wise man. He is so wise, Kli Ning doesn't understand half the things Guru Neverminda says. But Kli Ning tells us that we should get a detailed grip on the big picture. For instance, Guru Neverminda explained that we should spend much money on printing our customer charter and corporate mission statement. Kli Ning likes the idea of publicising our new way, but just doesn't like having to pay monastery taxes on idea dissemination."

Tai Tso was puzzled. "What is this customer charter of which you speak?"

Lo Fan grew even more excited and pressed a small, rumpled rice paper scroll into Tai Tso's hand. Tai Tso read aloud, "Her long, sensuous legs, wrapped around his massive..."

"...no, not that side. I am sorry, Kli Ning insisted that we use recycled paper from the monastery."

Tai Tso turned the scroll and again began to read:

> We, the dedicated laundry employees of the Kwik Klining Duck Tea House and Laundry, servants of the illustrious Chao Kli Ning, a wise and benevolent businessman with an uncanny knack for spotting an opportunity to make a quick buck, do hereby solemnly pledge to boldly strive at all times, and to the utmost of our ability to:
>
> ■ Every day, in every way, constantly contemplate our customers' requirements and seek our customers' guidance on innovative, entrepreneurial and totally satisfying ways to meet their needs
>
> ■ Endeavour to infinitely improve ourselves and honour our ancestors and thus, in so doing, produce the ultimate service for our community and in our small, modest way make the world in which we live a perfect place for not just ourselves or our immediate descendants but for infinite generations yet unborn
>
> ■ Give good laundry in an utterly excellent manner.

Tai Tso reflected for a few moments and then said, "This is truly an impressive customer charter. Why is this necessary?"

"Between you and me, Tai Tso, Guru Neverminda noticed that we have a few quality problems. Have you ever noticed an unpleasant smell?"

"Oh, hardly at all," said Tai Tso.

"Of course, we have a massive laundry here, employing more than forty staff. There are bound to be a few small quality problems – a slight odour, the occasional tear, a few minor mix-ups…"

"…like the day the whole village turned out in pink shirts?"

"Oh, that was a minor problem with our bleach. Anyway, I'm talking about more substantial matters. Guru Neverminda says that quality from Ti Ku should be free. By investing more time in avoiding problems, he says, we'll spend much less time correcting errors and losing customers," said Lo Fan.

"If I were upset with you, I would just ask my wife to do the laundry," said Tai Tso.

"That's precisely the point Guru Neverminda made. We must prevent quality failure by having a quality control process with inspection, standards and external review. For a modest fee, Guru Neverminda was prepared to lend us one of his Ti Ku disciples, Aiso. Aiso is busy hiring people for his quality inspectorate, producing procedures manuals, establishing performance standards, formulating quality measures and devising quality checklists. With Aiso's help, we expect to be able to break down and understand the individual components of quality in our laundry."

"None of this sounds free to me," said Tai Tso. "I couldn't see this Ti Ku stuff working at the noodle factory. People love our noodles without a quality control process. Anyway, can I have my laundry. I really need to get home."

When he got home, Tai Tso sorted his clean laundry and as usual found one or two of those irritating brown stains that were Kli Ning's trademark. Now that he knew that Lo Fan really cared, he felt it was his duty as a loyal customer to raise the matter with Lo Fan. On the morrow, the counter woman glumly handed Tai Tso a customer complaint form. He wanted to complete the form there and then, but was stymied on the first question: "Batch and reference number?" He took the form to the office and rummaged in the wastebasket for his old receipt. Lo Fan wasn't there when Tai Tso dropped off the form on his way home. The counter woman glumly accepted it and annoyingly said, "May the Ti Ku be with you."

Tai Tso met a cheery Lo Fan the next morning. Lo Fan thanked him profusely for taking the time to submit a properly completed complaint form, although Lo Fan indicated a few non-conformities where Tai Tso had failed to use the correct date format. Tai Tso bridled at Lo Fan's suggestion that he consider a refresher course on his handwriting.

"Lo Fan, this complaint is not about my handwriting," said Tai Tso. "What are you going to do about my laundry?"

"We're not sure that we have a problem yet, but let me tell you where we are in our investigation. Aiso was delighted that we now have an opportunity to deal with a real quality issue. Guru Neverminda says that receiving a customer complaint is half way to achieving the quality improvement of Ti Ku. Without complaints you cannot measure your progress. We're feeling better already."

"Yes, but what about the brown stains?"

"Ah, those," said Lo Fan, "so far, Aiso feels that we have followed our existing procedures perfectly. Most importantly, the stains were duly noted on the packing checklist. Nevertheless, Aiso believes that maybe our ironing checklist could go a bit further. There isn't a stain tick-box for ironing and Aiso blames himself totally for this unforgivable oversight. Guru Neverminda has even suggested that we consider including our quality checklist in your laundry bundles to demonstrate our commitment to quality. Once these minor improvements are made, Guru Neverminda assures us that we are close to knowing the components of quality."

"Lo Fan, I'm pleased that things are working so well for you, but what about the brown stains?"

"Oh, don't worry, now that we nearly have the process right, Guru Neverminda tells us that the content is sure to follow. Further, Aiso has suggested that we send a letter promptly to all complainants. You should receive yours within a week or so. Have a Ti Ku day."

Three weeks later, a disgruntled Tai Tso opened a letter from Kli Ning's laundry. "Thank you for your enquiry about the problems you may or may not be having with our laundry services. We are looking into this matter and will be in touch with you again as soon as possible. In the meantime, should you wish to contact us, be sure to quote your reference number above." The now even more disgruntled Tai Tso, having noted the prompt response, personal tone, individual attention to his problem and missing reference number, decided to have a little moan to Lo Fan.

"Lo Fan, your charter said that you would give good laundry in an utterly excellent manner. Three weeks have passed and now, if anything, the stains are getting worse. Certainly not better. In fact, you bring the stains to my attention each time Aiso includes a quality control checklist in my bundle."

"Oh, you are so wise to grasp the paradox between process and content.

I now understand why your noodle products are so well loved. Your noodles are consistent in length. We need to ensure that we give every customer a consistent laundry service. I can assure you that your laundry has gone through the same process as every other villager's. Guru Neverminda says that our enlightenment along the path of Ti Ku will go through many levels. At this level, we are putting the customer first. We need to understand what you really want."

"I want stain-free laundry," muttered Tai Tso.

"Of course you do. But you want far more besides – prompt and friendly service, value for money, professionalism and a hygienically conscious environment. We want this, because we know that many of our potential customers still prefer their wives to do the laundry, despite all of our expenditure on quality. For this reason, Guru Neverminda is leading us this very afternoon in a quality ring meditation on continuous improvement. We hope to understand better how our service can be tailored to our customers' needs, while still meeting our specifications. In fact, I meant to tell you that your laundry won't be ready until tomorrow because of the quality ring."

"What do you do in a quality ring? Is it like my wife's silk-spinning circle?" quipped an increasingly sceptical Tai Tso.

"Very similar," said Lo Fan, "you truly have an insight into these matters. The noodle factory must be very close to Ti Ku enlightenment. In our quality ring this afternoon, we hope to look beyond satisfying our service specifications and look forward to fulfilling our customers' innermost desires."

"How do customers get to attend one of your quality rings?"

"Guru Neverminda says that only by looking deep into ourselves can we truly understand our customers. It is important that we have prime time to meditate on our own. We are like believers who follow the form of their religion without understanding the way. We observe the fasts, the days of rest, the sexual strictures and some of the more enigmatic, traditional practices. We have a quality process, but are yet to achieve the enlightenment of Ti Ku."

"Why don't you just give the customers what they want? We give good noodles; why don't you simply give good laundry?" asked Tai Tso.

"How will we know when our laundry is high quality?"

Drawing from an exam question for his noodle inspector's certificate, Tai Tso asked, "Of all the grains of sand on the beach, which is the highest quality?"

Lo Fan was speechless, deep in thought. Tai Tso fidgeted nervously. He was fast losing patience with Lo Fan's evangelism and was seriously considering the advantages of getting his wife to do the laundry tomorrow. Suddenly Lo Fan burst forth. "You are truly a master of quality. Consistency isn't everything. I can see that the noodle factory must have long ago achieved Ti Ku. You never told me that you have been working with Guru Neverminda all these years."

"We have not worked with your Guru. Or any other Guru. We know what we're doing. We make good noodles. People want to buy them."

"Oh such wisdom, to measure quality through success. I now understand the true Way. Inspections, checklists and procedures can be obstacles to quality unless they are means to Z/Yen enlightenment. We need to do – what we do – well."

"Yes, but what about the brown stains?" concluded Tai Tso.

Two months later Tai Tso wanted to talk to Lo Fan about a small tear in one of his shirts. Tai Tso had heard about Guru Neverminda's hasty return to his secluded monastery in a not quite clean robe. There were murmurings in the village that Kli Ning's expected donation to the Guru's monastery had not been forthcoming. Further, Kli Ning had been heard to say to the abbot, "We need to get a big picture grip on the details" – a sure sign of his displeasure. Tai Tso had also heard of the paperwork minimisation procedures instituted by Aiso after his former master's departure. Tai Tso had to admit that some changes had been made. He appreciated not receiving those irritating checklists. Some days, he found fewer brown stains than usual. The stench remained unchanged. Lo Fan greeted Tai Tso warmly.

"Things are better, aren't they? Just say it Tai Tso," said Lo.

QUESTIONS FOR STUDENTS

Write an appropriate customer charter for the Kwik Klining Duck Tea House and Laundry's restaurant staff.

Design a laboratory test for Tai Tso's noodles which accurately measures their pre- and post-boiling elasticity. Use exact approximations where necessary.

WHITE SOCKS AND RED SOCKS
AND PINK SOCKS BETWEEN
LAUNDRY INSPECTOR'S STANDARD BOOK OF NURSERY RHYMES

WHEN ALL THE INFORMATION
TELLS A TALE, THE TAIL IS OF
BAD INFORMATION
SOUL OF A NEW ABACUS

THE QUESTION OF HU

Which reveals the essential thirst of all successful organisations for accurate information and reprographics, but which also reveals the inescapable fact that Chao Cha's intuition is superior to both.

"THAT LADY IS SURE all that glitters is gold," remarked Chung Lin to her beau, Lo Fan. Lin was referring to Chao Kli Ning's wife Cha.

Much as he loved and respected his fiancée Lin – the ex-wife of former restaurateur Chung Chong Chop – Lo Fan was incredulous. Lo Fan was, after all, the loyal manager of Chao Kli Ning's business empire, the Kwik Klining Duck Tea House and Laundry (a laundry and two restaurants). And Chao Cha was to be respected, indeed revered, by all of Chao Kli Ning's staff.

"What do you mean, Lin?" asked Lo Fan.

"She seems to assume that large bundles of clean laundry and vast quantities of food represent huge sums of money for her to spend. Her home makeover and landscape gardening ideas, which she insists on espousing at every public opportunity, such as our silk-spinning circle, beggar belief. I fail to see how a mere laundry and restaurant business could ever yield sufficient profits to meet such aspirations."

"Yet she seems to understand the complexity of measuring profit in intricate businesses like ours," said Lo Fan. "Funnily enough, earlier today I suggested to Kli Ning that we should encourage her to become more involved in the business, so she would appreciate our problems."

"What was Kli Ning's response to that idea?" asked Chung Lin.

Lo Fan emulated Chao Kli Ning's deep voice to emphasise the gruff quotation. "He said, 'Don't be absurd, Lo Fan, get a detailed grip on the big picture, that really was one of your less helpful ideas,' or words to that effect."

"That sounds like him," laughed Chung Lin.

On the other side of the village, the Chaos sat at dinner. "I think I should start to get more involved in the business," said Kli Ning's wife, Chao Cha. "I have certain intuitions about business which you seem to lack. For instance, I would never allow the figures to get so out of date that I wasn't sure what I had left to spend," she remarked pointedly.

Kli Ning recognised her mood. He had seen the same mood when she mentioned her intuitions about botany. He had been forced to hire a full-time gardener to help her intuit botany more accurately. He had seen the same mood just before she told everyone her intuitions about decorating their home. He had been forced to hire an interior designer to avoid some of her more extreme inspirations.

"Funnily enough," said Kli Ning, with only the slightest trace of hypocrisy, "I was just remarking to Lo Fan today that we might benefit from your involvement. I told Lo Fan that he should appreciate your help with our business problems. Just give me a day or two to hire you a personal information assistant."

"You are quite right, my husband," said Cha, "I have little enough time to spare even a moment crawling around in the details of your grubby business. But once I have a few meaningful facts and figures, I bet I can wring out enough extra cash to redecorate the house and landscape the garden."

Kli Ning knew he had little time and organised the interviews for Cha's assistant the next morning. By the following day he was down to a shortlist of two, Hu and Wen.

Kli Ning asked Hu and Wen the same question. "Can you give my wife all the information she wants?"

Wen immediately explained basic information theory, management by objectives, critical success factors and key performance indicators, drawing on pertinent examples and illustrating from personal experience. Kli Ning was impressed and knew that Wen would make an excellent management information officer.

The other candidate, Hu, paused before answering, "You can't always get what you want; but if you try sometimes, you just might find, you get what you need."[5] Kli Ning then knew he had found his wife's personal information

---

[5] Even to this day, in Guangzhou, the lyrics of a certain rock'n'roll band are strangely popular amongst middle-aged businessmen and management information officers.

assistant. Hu was hired and began to try pretty hard to find what Cha needed, although at times Hu's methods became a little extreme.

In his twilight years, Win Kin, the head calligrapher, had finally become fed up with the daily drudgery of copying by hand the menus, the laundry price lists, Ti Ku checklists, advertising leaflets, Kli Ning's business cards, Cha's charity pamphlets and all the other paraphernalia of ancient Eastern business life. Win Kin had a dream – the dream of calligraphic automation. After forty-five years of calligraphy, as a leading light in the Worshipful Company of Chartered Calligraphers, and as the revered developer of the flourish on Registered Character No. 2714, Win Kin still sought renown as a true revolutionary, seeking to shake the very foundations of calligraphy itself. Win Kin foresaw a brave new world: a world based on freedom of, and free access to, information; a world in which decisions could be based on timely and reliable printed matter; a world with leaflets describing new products and special offers, as available to the lowliest peasant as to the mightiest emperor; yea, a world where each household virtually bursts with newsrolls, coupons, journals, directories and unsolicited mail.

Meanwhile, Lo Fan had not got what he wanted, but was trying very hard to find it. For the last two weeks Lo Fan and Win Kin had stayed late every evening, sometimes until midnight, working on Win Kin's great idea in the basement of the laundry. Win Kin and Lo Fan had somewhat different objectives for their late work. Lo Fan was keen to speed up the calligraphy process, in particular the daily menus. Lo Fan always supported potential reductions in headcount. Naturally, Lo Fan knew that there were pressing grounds for completing Win Kin's calligraphic automaton before Win Kin's retirement. In fact, if he could get Win Kin to finish the calligraphic automaton within four weeks, Lo Fan could bundle Win Kin out to pasture six months early and avoid the need to pay a full retirement pension.

Cha didn't know what she wanted, but she was trying very hard to get Hu to find it. Certainly, she had some clear ideas on areas for improvement, starting with the high cost of sea bass. Cha didn't feel that it was appropriate to share these ideas with her conniving husband or his sycophantic hire Hu whom he had hired just for her. She realised that she still needed to think through some of the details, but knew that the areas for improvement included better revenue reporting, more detailed cost centre allocations and weekly sea bass prices. In short, Cha wanted more information.

Kli Ning was happy enough for the moment. Cha seemed pleased with Hu. Hu seemed capable of pleasing Cha. Hu also seemed to know on which side his bread was buttered; Hu reported daily to Kli Ning on Cha's latest caprice. Kli Ning also appreciated Lo Fan's special project. The details were a bit murky, but seemed to involve improved business processes, lower headcount and a reduced draw on the pension fund with the possibility of a future pension surplus. The staff were understandably a bit twitchy, because the new man Hu was wandering around asking questions, compiling reports, demanding rigorous accounts of how the staff had spent their time, extracting details on the taboo matter of sea bass payments and, worst of all, he spent an uncommon amount of time chatting to Kli Ning and Cha. In short, Hu was desperately short of information. The staff smelt trouble when they knew it. The customers, as is customary, noticed nothing.

Hu was having to scurry about more than he had expected when he glibly won the job. Cha was nearly as sharp as she tried to look. Hu understood Cha's revenue reporting requirements. Cost centre allocations between the two restaurants were a piece of cake, as were laundry cash flow forecasts, but despite his daily trips to the fish market, he was having great difficulty compiling a sea bass price index which fully reflected spot and forward prices, as well as Kli Ning's customary backhanders. Hu was struggling to reconcile the sea bass price index with the daily and weekly sea bass payment schedules which Kli Ning was reluctantly surrendering to Cha.

Although Hu had discovered, through his investigations, Lo Fan and Win Kin's contraption in the laundry basement, he remained unsure how to turn it to his advantage. It would have helped had Hu known what the machine was designed to do. The machine seemed decidedly unusual, to the point of being strange. Until he had a chance to confront Lo Fan with the details of expenditure on the contraption, Hu was keeping his analysis of "sundry/ miscellaneous" to a minimum, in the hope that Cha's attentions were occupied with his other submissions. Hu hoped either to gain Cha's favour for uncovering a significant area of cost reduction or to get a slice of Lo Fan's seemingly sophisticated venture.

Cha was bound to notice "sundry/miscellaneous expenses" sooner or later.

She asked, "O esteemed husband, would it be acceptable if I took sixty per cent of the business profits as pocket money for a little inspiration of mine?"

Kli Ning's reply was swift and firm. "My beloved wife, naturally such expenditure on a personal scheme would be completely untenable."

"I understand that, O revered husband. So can you explain to me the purpose of spending twenty per cent of our turnover, that being sixty per cent of our profit, on sundry/miscellaneous expenses? Surely I deserve an explanation?"

Kli Ning kicked himself for not taking adequate precautions sooner, but was grateful to Hu for keeping it under wraps so long. Kli Ning was even more grateful when Hu burst in, apparently unconnectedly.

"Get a look at this, O esteemed masters!" exclaimed Hu. He appeared to be waving an extraordinarily large pile of menus under the Chaos' noses. "Every menu is identical. We can produce dozens an hour!"

"Pity we don't have that many customers," muttered Kli Ning. Then a little louder, for Cha's benefit, "Ah, this is just like the Temple of Ten Thousand Identical Buddhas. Hu, what wonderful results from our sundry/ miscellaneous expense items."

"Oh dearest," said Cha, "I had no idea you were so far-sighted to understand the need for using profits in a well-developed research and development programme, well hidden from the prying eyes of tax inspectors. With this menu copying machine we can increase the number of customers; we can get rid of the calligraphy department; we can even reprint all the staff timesheets."

Kli Ning relaxed. Cha was now all sweetness and light. And Cha seemed pleased with her perceptive husband.

But Cha then demonstrated why she was justly famous for her mood swings. "However, if the two of you think that I can possibly work with such primitive management information, you have another thing coming. How can I possibly help you if you won't help yourselves? Imagine the absurdity. Vast amounts wasted on ill-defined research, piling enormous resources into sundry and miscellaneous, unappraised investments."

Cha was in full flow. "I insist that you, Hu, develop a complete, accurate, valid, timely and well-maintained management information system, so that I might finally get a grip on this fishy business. If you don't deliver, I'll have you gutted like the pusillanimous guppy you are." Both men quivered – Hu for his job, Kli Ning for his life.

And so Hu did deliver.

It was magnificent. Management information of gargantuan proportions spewed out daily. But as long as the top few pages reflected Cha's view of the business, Hu could keep her quite happy with any large pile of paper. Oh she was bright enough to catch on if he gave her the same pile each day, but then Hu had his very own printing machine courtesy of Lo Fan and Win Kin.

Win Kin was happy enough that he had been allowed to keep his machine, albeit hidden in the basement. Unfortunately, the price Cha demanded was that he dismissed all of his calligraphy assistants. Win Kin was also sad that his brave new world of information seemed to be mainly repetitive piles of paper for Hu's management information system. All technology seemed to be enlisted for the forces of the dark side. Such was progress.

Lo Fan was happy enough with the new efficiencies. He wasn't sure if the printing machine had been worth all the late nights, but he had to admit that Win Kin had produced a wondrous advance, possibly beyond that of the revered Registered Character No. 2714. Unfortunately, Lo Fan couldn't put the world's only printer out to pasture just yet and was having to pay Win Kin's full retirement pension as well as post-retirement wages. For some unexplained reason, the re-hired calligraphy assistants, now called printing apprentices in Hu's management information system, were more expensive than before they were fired. Such was progress.

But progress is often one step forwards, two steps back. The day the sea bass price quadrupled, Kli Ning knew that year's profit was doomed. The fish merchant's daughter's pre-paid wedding banquet called for two hundred covers of sea bass as the highlight of the meal. Hu had been so busy producing copious reports for Cha, he had lost track of their exposure to the great fish. This oversight was more galling as the sea bass future price was listed at line five of page one in Hu's daily report to Cha. Kli Ning could kick himself. Had he and Hu not been so busy humouring Cha, Kli Ning might have used the information and his ill-gotten contacts in wet fish to make a pile. Even better, Cha wouldn't have known. But Kli Ning didn't get that kind of luck.

Cha made her own luck. It was a complicated form of luck, largely involving arbitrage between spot and forward sea bass prices as well as two swaps through sea cucumber and abalone. Cha could hardly wait to tell Kli Ning about her enormous, crystallised gains in sea bass. She even thought perhaps Hu would deserve a bonus in two or three years, if he lasted that long. On the other hand she pondered, perhaps the Chaos deserved all the credit for employing Hu so effectively.

That evening, dinner at the Chaos was all sea bass and conversation. "Our profits this year should show some dramatic changes," Kli Ning ventured tentatively, pulling a stray bone from between his teeth.

Cha giggled, "Yes, there have been some significant market anomalies which could cause great good or ill, depending on your overall net exposure to wet fish."

Kli Ning, seeing the futility of concealing their trading losses, replied, "Naturally, some things being greater than others, although less than some, leave many positions in an area which could turn adverse under other circumstances, albeit not necessarily those which were encountered today. Does this make sense sweetheart? Which reminds me, I wanted to ask your advice about the two hundred sea bass for next Saturday's wedding banquet."

"Oh, definitely steamed with ginger and spring onion," replied Cha. "You cannot possibly get full credit for the fish if you drench it in black bean sauce. As for the price, our new management information system should ensure that you and Hu can make successful sea bass pricing decisions on your own. I'm a bit tired of trying to do everything. In fact, I feel that I should return to some interior decorating and spend more time with my silk-spinning circle. Anyway, now that you and Hu are focusing on the key items, I feel that our businesses are a bit more secure."

Kli Ning was a bit perplexed. "I'm not sure I want to count on too many successes like today's," he replied glumly. "Get a big picture grip on the details. Before you return to the important role of village socialite, perhaps you can explain how we can afford to buy two hundred sea bass next week?"

"I know it was expensive, but two thousand sea bass futures mean that we can supply next Saturday's banquet and pocket a net profit on eighteen hundred sea bass quadrupling in price," said Cha. "I hope you don't mind my last minute deal. You know I can't resist a bargain."

"Um eighteen hundred," replied Kli Ning eloquently. "You, um, I see."

"Oh, I'm sorry if I overstepped the mark," said Cha. "But you and Hu make it look so easy. All this buying and selling after you work out that ferociously complicated pile of management information. Especially as the supporting pages are so little help in understanding the top few pages. I just had to try it myself. I promise not to do it again."

As a pre-eminent businessman, Kli Ning possessed sufficient powers of recovery to insist, "See that it doesn't happen again. You know that only we know which information to focus on. I shall use Hu's printed information to invest your windfall gain wisely. Had I been privy to the information that you saw, I would have managed the risks and rewards the Z/Yen way, which would surely have netted more than eighteen hundred fish. All that glitters is not gold."

"O my beloved," chirped Cha, "I am delighted that you will now rely on proper information to run our business. But the profit on the sea bass is already committed to my home improvement project. You just won't believe the original feature I have designed for our garden..."[6]

QUESTIONS FOR STUDENTS

■ Prepare a simple generalised auto-regressive conditional heteroskedastic model of sea bass future prices cross-correlated with pork bellies.

■ Design a calligraphic character which you could register and would qualify you to join the Worshipful Company of Calligraphers. Now try to figure out what it means.

---

[6] Even to this day, in Shenzen province, constructing a pagoda is known colloquially as "buying a stairway to heaven."

7

A MAN WHO KNOWS HIS NUMBERS HAS
TAKEN ONLY HALF A STEP BACKWARDS

MUNG, ADUKI AND SOYA: THE HISTORY OF BEAN COUNTING

NEVER LOOK A MAD MONK IN THE
MOUTH, HE MIGHT HAVE HALITOSIS.
BUT DO LISTEN, HIS WORDS MIGHT
CHANGE THE COURSE OF YOUR LIFE

(BELIEVED TO BE FROM) THE BOOK OF CHAO KLI NING

BROTHERS IN ALMS

Containing a parable of life, the universe and augmenting a bank account through the power of faith.

CHAO KLI NING RUSHED BACK from the laundry to his home. He had only half an hour to get packed and moving or he would not make it to the first staging post before nightfall. The staging post was on the road to Guilin, the city of hills, karsts, rivers and nocturnal pleasures. He could hardly wait to be on the road. After all, this was his annual business trip. His only regret was that, as usual, his untrustworthy staff at the laundry and two restaurants had needed an entire morning of discipline before he felt comfortable leaving them in charge. He was hardly in the right frame of mind for an enlightening journey in search of innovative ideas and invigorating, competitive, self-analysis – in short, a business trip.

During the flurry of packing, Cha, Kli Ning's wife, entered their room. "My esteemed and beloved husband, surely you cannot leave our Kwik Klining Duck Tea House and Laundry alone for so many weeks while you travel on this ludicrous 'business trip'. Neither of us trusts the staff to run the places properly

when you are away. Last time, they so insulted the food inspector that you spent six months wining and dining the entire inspectorate in our restaurants for free, to prevent the inspector from revoking our licences on health grounds."

"Don't be absurd, Cha. That sort of thing won't happen again. This time, I have left very clear instructions. Besides, this business trip is essential. Get a detailed grip on the big picture. Without this trip, we may fall behind in catering and cleaning standards. This particular conference in Guilin only happens every three years. With this year's theme, 'How to Clean Up in Feasts', my colleagues have insisted that I present a paper on the future of bleach in laundry and catering. I simply must go, and I am going."

And so he did. Kli Ning breezed out of the house with his baggage. His mood visibly improved as he passed through the gateway followed by a slightly overburdened donkey, struggling to carry copies of Kli Ning's paper, produced by Win Kin's automated calligraphy machine in Kli Ning's laundry basement.

In the long shadows of dusk, not so far from Kli Ning's first staging post, an unassuming monk wheezed along the road. The monk's breathing was the least of his problems. His legs were bowed, his back bent, his face had seen better days. In short, there was little time to make it to the staging post before nightfall – and possibly even less time after that. It was then that the monk took a wrong turn, heading through the bush for two hours before popping out, exhausted, right in Kli Ning's path, in the twilight.

"Greetings, old brother," hailed Kli Ning, as night began to fall. "It gets dark in these hills quickly, doesn't it?" Kli Ning remembered well the old superstition of helping the first needy person one meets when setting out on a journey.

The monk wheezed a little by way of reply.

Taking the wheeze as a good sign, Kli Ning tried again. "Brother, I have just started on my journey and left our village only a few hours ago, but I think you might find that it is too far to go without light. Perhaps you would accompany me to the staging post up the road, where I intend to spend a restful night?"

The monk managed to gasp, "Thank you, young man. May the blessings of the wheel of fortune spin in your favour."

"Oh," said Kli Ning, "from your blessing I assume that you belong to the Brothers in Alms. I see more and more of your fellow monks in our village. Your sect must be doing well."

Kli Ning only just heard the monk's response, which seemed to lack reverent modesty. "You bet we're doing well," panted the monk.

"Yes, brother. Anyway, I am Chao Kli Ning, restaurateur, launderer and businessman. I am on a business trip to Guilin, presenting a paper at an important conference."

"I am Alm, founder of Brothers in Alms, former master of the order until my ungrateful acolytes decided that they knew a better way."

"Yes, I know how you feel. If my laundry and restaurant managers pursued their better ways, they would have thrown me out long ago. Let me help you onto the donkey. We can talk some more when we get to the staging post." Kli Ning wondered about the identity of his fellow traveller on the way to the staging post. If he truly was Alm, why was he here alone at night? However, the fame of Alm was such that only a fool would try to impersonate the great monk, perhaps bringing untold misfortune upon himself. And what did Alm mean by "ungrateful acolytes"?

After supper, Kli Ning and the monk shared a room. Kli Ning felt he would either gain grace by paying the bill or save money by splitting the bill. The monk knew in his soul that he would not need to pay his half of the bill. The monk droned on immodestly for a while, then suddenly fell into a snoring sleep. Kli Ning found it difficult, but managed to get to sleep over the monk's strained breathing. Kli Ning dreamed vividly and seemed to feel a tapping on his shoulder. When he turned around to look in his dream, he saw the monk floating cross-legged, six inches off the floor.

"The wheel of fortune is unlucky for some. Such is my ill luck that a mere businessman shall be my final confessor. You, Kli Ning, shall hear my life's tale and assist me in the next turn of the wheel. I shall make my final confession to you."

In his dream, Kli Ning sensed the monk's frustration and lack of humility. Kli Ning felt the passing of millennia, the rise and fall of great faiths. He imagined some complex future religion where this notion of guilt and confession formed the basic tenets of faith, in conjunction with long pilgrimages, strictures on dietary habits, tortuous reproductive logic and fanatical beliefs in everlasting, interminable rebirth rather than a quiet, decisive death. Kli Ning made a mental note to try and forget these horrors when he awoke.

What a dream! The monk continued, "Forgive me brother, for I have sinned. At first I was a truly devout monk of my order. I kept my silence. I did not crave wealth and power, nor fame and riches, nor fortune and favour, not even money. I didn't like the early hours, the cold gruel, the silence or the hard floors but I believed that my brothers and I were having a good time. I accepted that this lifestyle was the way to enlightenment. Later I became disillusioned with our lack of focus. We sought to enlighten all mankind, but when our brethren sought our advice, we remained silent. I began, tentatively, to advise some of our donors in whispers. In the beginning my advice didn't stick, although my fame grew as the only local talking monk. Rather than chastising me for breaking silence, my abbot realised that we had more donors than any neighbouring monastery and he encouraged me to continue."

"But still I was frustrated. The same people kept returning each week with the same problems unsolved. How could I truly help them? My first major sin was losing my temper with an old woman when she returned for the umpteenth time posing the question 'Does my budgerigar have a soul?' I was about to answer for the umpteenth time, 'Does a sparrow sing with swallows in summer?' but I realised that repetition would not help the old woman. I lost my temper, 'If you really want the answer to that question, pledge all your belongings to my abbot,' knowing that she would bother me no more. She ran away surprisingly quickly for a woman of her age. To my astonishment she returned the same day with a deed of transfer to the abbot. She asked me her question again. Again I replied, 'Does a sparrow sing with swallows in summer?' The old woman sighed and walked away peacefully, apparently satisfied. I knew I had discovered a deep secret, but I wasn't sure what it was."

Kli Ning pinched himself, failed to wake up, shrugged, and then interjected, "But surely it's not a sin to charge people for good advice?"

The monk continued virtually seamlessly. "The abbot told me I had sinned because never had we told a donor the amount they should give. He threw me out of the monastery for my presumption. I left and wandered the region. I pondered my misdeeds. I realised that I should have charged the woman more; she had wealthy relatives. I also realised that people value advice more, the more they are charged for it. I resolved to found a new order to help people to help themselves by charging them significant amounts of money for advice. I founded the Brothers in Alms." With his legs still crossed, the monk hovered out into the garden of the staging post.

Kli Ning followed the floating monk into the garden and asked, "So you lost your temper and told an old woman how much she should pay. Surely that is not so great a sin, especially as such great good flowed from your behaviour?"

"Oh losing my temper wasn't the sin, the sin came from the temptation of money. When I founded Brothers in Alms, I wanted to be sure of controlling the quality of our work. I insisted that the brothers donate a portion of their donations to me. From this I established a personal monastery. I insisted that monks came for regular briefings and retraining in our Way. I wrote our order's book, *Advice Ain't Easy if it's Free.* Many people, including that old woman, spread our fame far and wide."

Kli Ning burst in here, anxious to participate in what was, after all, his own dream. "Yes, your local brothers are the most expensive advice givers in my area. I would happily pay for quality advice, although maybe not theirs, but I still don't see the big sin. What of a little temptation and your own monastery?" Kli Ning wished his theological underpinnings weren't quite so rusty.

The monk returned to his life's tale. "You are so right. A little pyramid monkery business is not new. The new part was the idea of compensation for using the order's insignia, begging bowls, uniforms, walking sticks, official song scrolls, prayer oil, sandals, incense, holy bells and sacred books. We made a packet. It exceeded my wildest expectations. I had never understood the power of brand image; that was my temptation, and my downfall."

Kli Ning was aghast. "You mean you franchised our deepest beliefs in the fundamental concepts of existence in order to make some extra money for your personal monastery?"

The monk seemed indignant, especially for a person humbly reviewing his life before a stranger. "How dare you question my motives? Get a big picture grip on the details. I was helping people. People just hadn't spent enough on helping themselves before. I made it easy. My monks made it easier. Our franchising system worked and we prospered. You, a mere businessman, cannot comprehend the subtle workings of religion."

The monk's voice began to rise and a far away look entered his eyes. "I had influence. I had real power. For a while, the emperor himself consulted me on the course of his life daily. I established some teaching seminaries. We manufactured our own prayer wheels for all our prayer wheel halls. I had plans for a chain of rest monasteries. I even had overseas rights. I tried all these things: seminaries, the monastery chain, prayer wheel manufacturing, overseas operations. We lost a packet, but I could have been a contender!" The monk's mind seemed to wander a bit and he began to drool.

Kli Ning had had enough. In his disgust, Kli Ning broke a branch from the banyan tree in the garden and chased the monk down the road, "Begone from my dreams, you mercenary monk; you, you avaricious abbot, you failed friar, begone."

Kli Ning woke in a sweat. Without turning over to see his roommate, Kli Ning knew he shared the room with a corpse. After some expensive arrangements with the innkeeper, Kli Ning managed to pack. He lamented the inconvenient demise of the monk, not just because he had to pay the full room charge. He hoped he had gained some extra grace from these unfortunate proceedings, particularly from covering the funereal charges for a penniless evangelist. Kli Ning wanted to believe deep, deep down that this costly experience must have been good for his soul.

As Kli Ning left the staging post, followed by his overburdened donkey, he looked at the garden and noticed the branch which he dreamt of breaking in that strange dream, save that the branch was in reality... well, broken. Now Kli Ning was sorely troubled. He pondered the strange dream of the night before, certain that the dream had little significance. Or had it been a dream? The previous night unnerved him and he wondered if he was in the right frame of mind for an enlightening business trip.

As he pondered, Kli Ning became indignant. The very thought of a penniless monk calling him, Chao Kli Ning, proprietor of the Kwik Klining

Duck Tea House and Laundry, "a mere businessman". He, the owner of the largest laundry in his region. Indeed, the only laundry in the region. And he, Chao Kli Ning, owner of surely two of the largest restaurants in all China. And he had plans. Big plans. A second laundry perhaps. After that, who knows, perhaps a third restaurant. No one called Chao Kli Ning "a mere businessman", not even in his wildest dreams. And certainly not some deranged monk who probably couldn't even run a tea stall, let alone a restaurant. In fact, that stupid old monk probably couldn't have even, what did he call it, "franchised" a tea stall, let alone a restaurant. Then the big idea hit Chao Kli Ning. This was big time Z/Yen enlightenment. Franchise the Kwik Klining Duck Tea House and Laundry. Kli Ning was going to be a contender.

QUESTIONS FOR STUDENTS

Would you expand the Kwik Klining Duck Tea House and Laundry through organic growth, acquisition, franchising, war or merger with an already established religion?

Do you believe, do you really believe, do you really really believe or do you believe at all? Just testing.

WHEN THE MIGHTY WHALE IS
DRAGGED DOWN, IT IS BY A BILLION
REPLICATING MICROBES FEASTING
STUDIES IN MICROBIOLOGICAL CULINARY TASTE

IF YOU'VE GOT IT, FLAUNT IT
(SAID TO BE FROM) THE SAYINGS OF ALM

GREEKS HAVE A GENERAL WORD FOR IT

Documenting, at great length, a comprehensive mechanism for dealing with the future. Said mechanism being so comprehensive that documentation is unnecessary.

CHAO KLI NING WAS VERY, VERY HAPPY. The grass was greener, the skies were bluer, the smile on Kli Ning's face was oh so bright. His face was even brighter when he reviewed his general ledger. The general ledger positively glowed with debits and credits. Kli Ning was a bit unsure what these debits and credits meant, but there seemed to be a lot of them. Lo Fan assured him that it was mostly good news.

Despite the confusion over this new method of tracking business, Kli Ning knew that franchising worked. All over the region, every town and village within a day's ride had a Kwik Klining Duck Tea House And Laundry. Unfortunately, Kli Ning's village was a bit remote, so a day's ride only meant eight franchises. But he had big ideas.

Lo Fan was very, very troubled. He came to see Kli Ning about his worries. "I want to be completely honest, open and straightforward with you, Kli Ning. Frankly, this could be difficult."

"What's going to be difficult?" asked Kli Ning.

"Being completely honest, open and straightforward, of course," replied Lo Fan.

"Don't worry about that. Just tell me what's on your mind," said Kli Ning in his kind voice.

"Well, O most esteemed one," began Lo Fan. "As you know our general ledger tells us many tales."

"Too many tales. Every time I read the ledger I seem to see each transaction twice!"

"That's because we enter them twice. Once on each side. Just like the Yen monks showed us. They call it duplicate entry."

"I call it double-effort bookkeeping," muttered Chao Kli Ning. "But what is the tale you read?"

"I am concerned about the tale of the future, O most esteemed one," ventured Lo Fan. "Our future is written in the scripts of our history. The rise and fall of whole economies is recorded in untold transactions. Yet the future is like an empty ledger, waiting to be filled. There is not yet a single entry, let alone a duplicate."

"Thus is the future different from the present, Lo Fan," said Kli Ning. "But surely these philosophical questions do not concern us now. As you can see, the Kwik Klining Duck Tea House and Laundry franchise scheme flourishes beneath our enlightened management."

"O most esteemed one, surely was never a truer word spoken. Your management is amongst the most enlightened that civilised man has had the good fortune to experience. Yea, even the ledgers bear testimony to your munificence. But the eight franchisees worry, and some even fret, for the future holds many terrors. The men want a plan."

"Get a big picture grip on the details. We'll tell the franchisees not to worry. This will make them feel better, especially as I have so clearly told them. This is my plan. Send each man a message confirming my prediction."

"As you command, so it shall be done," murmured Lo Fan, not altogether convincingly. "On your advice, I shall tell the franchisees not to worry."

The days passed. The bookkeeping entries doubled. The franchisees grew restless. They told Lo Fan that they felt the Kwik Klining Duck Tea House and Laundry chain lacked direction. Where would the new franchises be established? Was the slogan "Starching, pressing and a Kwik cup of tea while you wait? You've got it!" appropriate in every village in the region? Did all product names benefit from the suffix Chao, e.g. Duck Chao, Cow Chao, Tao Chao (monk's noodles), Now Chao (instant noodles) and Bao Wao Chao? Would regional demographics support a sustained rise in average household consumption amongst middle-income, dual-wage earning agricultural families? Did Kli Ning really have a plan? Lo Fan decided to tell Kli Ning another tale from the general ledger.

"Things are not going so well, O esteemed master," Lo Fan informed Kli Ning.

"Ah, so the tales from the ledger are not good. Tell me the problem," demanded Kli Ning.

"There is a far-off country, away to the west, where there are many strange thoughts, and stranger men. This land is called Greece, and the people Greeks. They fight many pointless battles and spend little time making money or spending it. A general who leads these pointless battles is called a 'strategos', for that is his function. The strategos is responsible for the disposition of the troops. Thus is the importance of these things understood."

"Are you saying that just because we have a little downturn in profit that we should start wars and build a market in imported generals?" asked Kli Ning, positively perplexed. "Perhaps you could be a bit clearer, Lo Fan?"

"The men want a strategy."

"First the men want a plan, now the men want a strategy. I want them to make up their minds."

"They say you should make up your mind and tell them the strategy, just like one of those foreign generals," pushed Lo Fan.

"Get a detailed grip on the big picture, Lo Fan," declared Kli Ning. "I shall think about the franchisees' concerns. However, we really don't have time for these long-term strategies and crazy foreign generals."

But Kli Ning did think long and hard on these exotic matters at his favourite riverside gazebo. He imagined himself as the head of a great army, conquering whole regions with new duck recipes and innovative stain-removing techniques. He fantasised pitched battles where his franchisees wrestled to the death with in-bred village restaurateurs, local government health officials and imperial tax collectors. When he emerged from his reverie, he summoned his scribe and dictated his vision. He then summoned Lo Fan to the riverside to hear his words.

In Xianatu village did Chao Kli Ning a stately strategy decree. Thus spake Chao Kli Ning to Lo Fan:

> My name is Chao Kli Ning, businessman of businessmen. Look on my franchises ye mighty and despair! The Art of War is a matter of vital importance to business – the road to survival or ruin. It is mandatory that it be thoroughly studied, otherwise you miss opportunities to make a quick buck.

At this point, Lo Fan broke into a cold sweat and wondered whether he had done the right thing by bullying his master into thinking about generals and long-range planning. Would he, Lo Fan, be held responsible for Kli Ning's delusions? Kli Ning continued, "There will be five fundamental factors upon which our glorious victories will be founded:

- The business of war is our business

- Our business is feeding and clothing

- The business of war gives us armies to feed and clothe

- Our franchisees are our front line

- Let's make war.

Kli Ning handed his scroll to Lo Fan with the words, "Now we've held our council standing beside this river gate. I am pleased and satisfied with my strategy. Chao Kli Ning has spoken. Now, Lo Fan, disseminate my words to the franchisees."

So Lo Fan toured the province, visiting each franchisee with Kli Ning's proclamation. Lo Fan did his best to explain Kli Ning's words to the franchisees. No one could quite comprehend the strategy, but all agreed it must be something to do with business acquisitions, possibly hostile bids. Most franchisees disagreed with making war, and a few felt that making love could be equally profitable and rewarding, as well as potentially more fun.

Lo Fan returned to Kli Ning with his findings. "O mighty one," he began, "your stately strategy decree has been most enlightening and has led to further enquiries. Also, I humbly beg to report that your franchisees feel that they've had no chance to contribute to such an important document, no chance to debate the issues and no chance to affirm their commitment to a strategy of acquisition. For instance, most of your obedient and humble franchisees think that business acquisitions stink. Good acquisitions are hard to find, consume too much time, lead to resentment and rarely work. The franchisees have made up their minds. They want a different strategy."

Kli Ning grew sorely frustrated at this. "If they want a different strategy they can have one. But they can do it themselves." Kli Ning started to walk away. Then he turned back to Lo Fan. "But if they do decide to do it themselves you'd better watch them like a hawk."

Lo Fan worked hard over the ensuing month. He felt like a camel trader trying to keep his dromedaries out of a Cantonese cooking pot. Lo Fan gained contributions to the strategy from visiting the franchisees. He developed a consensus through workshops with the franchisees and as the end of the month approached, he summoned all the franchisees to the village to meet with each other and gain their commitment before presenting the final strategy to Kli Ning.

The air was festive in the village hall where the franchisees assembled. Kli Ning struggled to remember names, although he had an uncanny memory for dishes served at a table where he was picking up the bill. Lo Fan also struggled to remember the franchisees names, a problem further exacerbated by Kli Ning's insistence on nicknaming the franchisees by the food they ate. Seeing the franchisees all gathered together for the first time, Lo Fan realised that consensus amongst these eight would be problematic, not least in agreeing the menu for meals during the day. He called the roll:

- Blood Pudding (dressed in leather armour, chanting war cries)
- Steamed Carp (desperately reading philosophical scrolls on Taoist business cycles)
- Drunken Chicken (nursing his bottle, dreaming of riches, occasionally yelling "hear hear")
- Double-Cooked Pork (currently reviewing the forty-seventh draft of his personal strategy)

- Seven-Treasures Duck (documenting every utterance, to ensure that the eventual strategy reflected all opinions)
- Spare Rib (arguing with everyone, using the single argument "keep it simple, stupid")
- Tofu (timidly refraining from all discussion, except the occasional, almost inaudible "no comment")
- Shark's Fin (convinced that the whole exercise was futile, but revelling in an all-expenses paid trip to Kli Ning's village).

The meeting was long and drawn out. It lasted most of the day. It would have lasted longer, but Drunken Chicken fell asleep and lightened Lo Fan's load. Shark's Fin excused himself and went to visit one of his cousins in the village. Lo Fan kept Double-Cooked Pork and Seven-Treasures Duck busy with notes, counter-notes, minutes and draft revisions. All seemed well, and Lo Fan had a slight sense of satisfaction as the day drew to a close. Then Kli Ning entered the hall. "Show me this new strategy upon which we have wasted so much time and money!" he demanded. The seven remaining franchisees and Lo Fan hastily assembled a presentation. They produced amazing pie charts, stunning matrix analyses and intricate financial projections. These proved beyond all reasonable doubt, to all but the most unbiased observer, that organic growth through franchising and territorial conquest was infinitely superior to acquisitions.

Kli Ning was truly astonished. "I am truly astonished," he exclaimed. "I never thought that you could develop a strategy on your own, especially one with no need for acquisitions. However, this seems very similar to my old strategy of waging metaphorical war on our business opponents. Nevertheless, I am indisputably pleased with our progress and resolve that we shall all henceforth adhere, without divergence of any sort whatsoever, to our chosen path and achieve the profitable conquest we all so richly deserve."

Drunken Chicken burped in agreement and the mood of the entire meeting was one of hearty self-congratulation. Shark's Fin burst in to share in Kli Ning's celebratory round of free drinks. Unfortunately Shark's Fin also burst out with an announcement that his village cousin knew of two particularly exciting restaurants less than two days journey away that had their own self-contained laundry facilities. Both these restaurants were ripe for acquisition. All the franchisees grew excited. Kli Ning grew even more excited. As Shark's Fin explained the details, Kli Ning knew that this was an acquisition opportunity too good to miss.

It was a confused Lo Fan who left the village hall late that night. Perhaps it was the drink, but Lo Fan felt that something was wrong. They had all worked hard for over a month on a detailed strategy. They had all finally agreed the principles, even Kli Ning. Then in one night they had thrown it all away to chase the latest exciting opportunity that had come their way, even though it violated their principle of non-acquisition. For many days, Lo Fan did not recognise the inner emotion which troubled him. If he had been a religious man, and not a businessman, he might have recognised "opportunity guilt" sooner. Lo Fan would have felt guilty had they not jumped at the acquisition opportunity. Instead, he now felt guilty for not following the strategy. The guilt was unavoidable. If Lo Fan had been a religious man, he could have made a lot of money selling this concept. Instead, it was to be many generations until Z/Yen scholars were to profit from enlightening others with the concept of "opportunity guilt".

As it was, thanks to all the changes of strategy and the paid expenses, the franchisees were reinvigorated and increased their earnings. Kli Ning's coffers grew with his share. The tales from the ledger improved. The strategy was safely framed on each franchisee's wall. Each franchisee fondly remembered the arguments they had had agreeing the strategy and referred to the arguments often when making new decisions.

Kli Ning also had the framed strategy on his wall. Kli Ning referred to the strategy often – too often – when making new decisions. He often used arguments from the strategy to justify his decisions. Kli Ning could never remember the actual arguments, as they were from sessions he had not attended. Kli Ning sometimes wondered what would have happened had they stuck to the strategy, without the acquisitions. The results of his acquisitions would take many more months to reveal themselves. There had been so many interesting ideas in the presentations at the village hall that night (known in Chao circles as "The Night of the Long Range Planning and Kitchen Knives"); ideas which wouldn't be tested in the heat of business battle.

Every time Kli Ning regarded the strategy on his wall, he asked himself "What does the future hold for my businesses?" The grass seemed browner, the sky seemed greyer. Kli Ning frowned as he pondered the future. But Kli Ning was a man with a strategy. Chao Kli Ning was very, very worried.

- Design a workshop for Chao Kli Ning, Lo Fan and the franchisees which would lead to all workshop delegates eventually barn dancing in matched pairs, with or without odd numbers of delegates.

- Opportunity guilt is the same feeling as the feeling one has when remaining faithful to one's spouse. Discuss (at home).

A STRATEGY? SELL MORE. SPEND LESS.
HAVE A BIG, ALL-EMBRACING, LUCRATIVE,
FOOLPROOF BUSINESS IDEA
A MANTRA FROM THE BROTHERS IN ALMS

AN HONOURABLE REPUTATION
CANNOT BE BOUGHT.
GOOD REPUTATION
FLOWS FROM GOOD DEEDS
OF GOOD CHARACTER.
MORALS ARE FOR SHEEP.
DO YOU HAVE ANYTHING
TO REMOVE THESE
MUTTON CHAO STAINS
FROM MY SHIRT?
OVERHEARD IN A CONVERSATION BETWEEN THE AGEING CONFUCIUS
AND THE YOUNG CHAO KLI NING, CIRCA 480 BC

KLI NING'S PRINCIPLE PROBLEM

During which Kli Ning discovers the risks of professional advice, the rewards of loyalty, the thrills of Seasonally Adjusted Transitional Employment Subsidy and the agonies of state bureaucracy.

THE MINUTE CHAO KLI NING walked into the joint you could tell he was a man of distinction. Chao Kli Ning owned the biggest business in the whole region: the 200 establishment strong Kwik Klining Duck Tea House and Laundry Franchise. Every village in the region either had a Kwik Klining or wanted one badly. Xianatu was the headquarters of the Kwik Klining empire. Kli Ning now employed so many people that the latest census decreed Xianatu officially a town – no longer the mere village of Chao Kli Ning's birth.

The joint into which he walked was the newly built town hall. The joint from which Chao Kli Ning walked, in a truly foul mood, should have been called "Newly-built-but-Yet-to-be-Paid-for-Town Hall." Kli Ning had just had a meeting with a number of men of consequence. The consequence was that these men of little distinction, namely local government officials, were going to cost Kli Ning a lot of money in extra taxes. These taxes would start to pay for, amongst other things, inspectorates, employment ministries, regulators and

naturally the mortgages on buildings such as the town hall to house them all.

These bureaucrats were also going to cost Kli Ning's human resources manager, Ai Char, even more time and effort in form filling and query chasing. The Regional Statistics Office had just reviewed Kli Ning's last quarter's forms and were demanding even more information.

That evening, Kli Ning dumped the new regulations on the desks of both Ai Char and his general manager, Lo Fan, with a message to meet him first thing the next morning. When the three met the following morning, Kli Ning was still in a foul mood. Lo Fan made it worse. "These new rules are preposterous. We'll have to keep records of all staff activities to the nearest minute. We couldn't do it accurately even if we tried. Those government officials couldn't use the information even if they got it."

Ai Char added to Kli Ning's gloom by beginning to indulge in his favourite pastime, quoting local government regulations. "Regulation 580/451 — Registered Character Number 4876 clearly requires us to submit complete, accurate and timely timesheets."

As usual, Lo Fan began to argue with Ai Char. "The last time you quoted regulation numbers at us, Ai Char, you tried to make us give tea breaks to our staff that were as long as those of our customers."

Ai Char interjected, "Lo Fan, you know as well as I that there are a lot of regulations to keep up with. That particular instance was an honest mistake confusing the interpretation of tea break contained in Regulation 1195/454 — Tea Break (Amendment) with the definition of staff tea breaks contained in

Regulation 37/455."

Kli Ning motioned them to stop. "Ai Char, Lo Fan. Get a big picture grip on the details. Are you telling me that we need to implement timesheets for all staff just to satisfy a bunch of petty, local bureaucrats who don't even have the wherewithal and taste to dine in my fine establishments?"

For once Lo Fan and Ai Char were in agreement and much against all their better wishes, they bought a timesheet recording system from leading experts at the Temple of Temporal Discontinuity. Strangely, Kli Ning began to appreciate the purchase some months later when Lo Fan called an urgent meeting. Lo Fan began, "I have been reviewing these timesheets and, oddly, the bureaucrats may have inadvertently helped us to save some money. It would appear that our headquarters staff are slightly inefficient. We should be able to fire half of them without noticing the slightest difference in service."

"Brilliant, Lo Fan," said Kli Ning expectantly, "how is this possible?"

"Well," began Lo Fan, looking from Kli Ning to Ai Char to his notes, "since we introduced timesheets we have had a few problems. Some staff complained that they had to spend more time filling in timesheets than they spent working. If you remember, you have already fired them. Our current problem is that most staff record most of their work time as non-productive. We have a code called 'waiting for work'. Junior staff record most of their time to this code. Senior staff complain that junior staff are either too busy to help or haven't prepared the senior staff work properly. Hence, the senior staff record almost all of their time to 'preparing for work'. Yet, whenever I talk to the junior staff, they claim that they spend all their spare time preparing the senior staff for work by doing the ledger calculations, filling in the senior staff forms, preparing the management accounts and fetching tea for the senior staff while they are 'waiting for work'. Thus the senior staff are doing the junior work, and the junior staff the senior work. We only need the senior staff work so we should fire them."

"Lo Fan," ventured Kli Ning, "as your brilliance often escapes me, perhaps you can explain how we can fire the junior staff and still have someone to fetch tea for the senior staff?"

"O esteemed master," continued Lo Fan, "as you have so perceptively seen, we don't fire the junior staff – we fire the senior ones! The timesheets prove that the junior staff are doing all the work."

"Lo Fan, that is brilliant," said Kli Ning. "Let us do this forthwith."

Ai Char coughed slightly to gain attention and then began, "This is truly insightful, but it is important to analyse thoroughly before considering such drastic action as actually firing people. Further, some of the technical regulatory issues concerning the employment of breadwinners, compulsory notice and form-filling staff ratios need to be confirmed before a satisfactory course of action can be put into a category for pending deliberation. I am personally disturbed at being the human resources manager of a firm which is about to fire half of its key staff and force them and their families into the streets, starving and without a realistic hope of re-employment in the locality. If you will permit me an evening's perusal of the regulations, I may be able to satisfy the regulations, halve the staff wages bill and yet keep all the staff on board."

Ai Char returned a bit bleary the next morning and explained a some-what convoluted scheme. Apparently, Kli Ning and Lo Fan had been unaware of Regulation 728/455 — Seasonally Adjusted Transitional Employment Subsidy. This regulation was meant to subsidise farmers so that they could employ their workers during the months between planting and harvest. The farmers simply registered their crop cycle periods and collected money from the government to pay their workers for the registered period between planting and harvest, known as "idle period". If Kli Ning registered his business as monthly seasonal and designated the middle two weeks of each month as "idle period", he could collect half the money for his staff bill from the government and not need to fire a soul.

Ai Char had even prepared a brief memo on the subject, which ended with the following conclusive paragraph: "Regulation 728/455 would appar-ently be potentially appropriate in this instance so far as the particulars have been established. Nevertheless, certain other consequences may or may not be of adequate significance to result in further consideration or consultation through a proper feasibility study."

After a few seconds of discussion, Kli Ning concluded with, "Well, that settles it. Let's do it." Even so, Kli Ning felt a deep unease in the place where his conscience occasionally deigned to reside. It was as if his stomach was telling him that it seemed immoral to pay people a full wage for what was clearly partial work. But he soon got over this feeling. The money was coming from the government and they paid people for partial work all the time. Sometimes the government even paid people for no work at all.

Some months later, not so far away, in the bowels of the town's new statistical office, an earnest clerk, Min, made a great discovery. His discovery was of such magnitude that it might even finish paying for the sparkling new government building in which Min worked. Indeed, it might also provide enough seed money to lay the foundations of another new building for another new department which might justify an increased budget and naturally some additional taxes. Min had uncovered what appeared to be a breach of Regulation 728/455 – Seasonally Adjusted Transitional Employment Subsidy.

Min had verified the chop used on the Kwik Klining Duck Tea House and Laundry Franchise's applications for Seasonally Adjusted Transitional Employment Subsidy. The applications were made by a certain Ai Char, a so-called human resources manager of the firm. Yet much to Min's surprise, the chop was registered to a certain Lo Fan, who listed his employment as general manager of the same firm. In accordance with normal procedures, Min raised an Initiation of Investigation for Criminal Fraud form against the aforementioned Lo Fan, published a Notice of Almost Certain Culpability and Criminal Activity against the Kwik Klining Duck Tea House and Laundry in the *Journal of Obscure Government Public Announcements,* passed the form to the most inappropriate department and promptly forgot all about it.

Eighteen bureaucrats later, the investigating official, Chih, sighed, hastily grabbed his regulations, slowly finished his cup of tea and somewhat languidly set off in the direction of Kli Ning's offices. On the way, Chih grabbed two police officers to help him with his enquiries in this informal investigation.

The three of them arrived at Kli Ning's offices and were greeted by Ai Char. After pausing for a cup of tea with Ai Char, they demanded to see Lo Fan immediately. Within minutes, Kli Ning was embroiled in debate. When the voices got too loud, Ai Char managed to convince everyone to sit calmly around the boardroom table and discuss the matter.

Chih explained the gross violation of Clause 328, the disparity between the submitter (Ai Char) and chopper (Lo Fan) of the applications. Kli Ning turned to Ai Char and asked him to explain. Chih raised his voice again, "You don't seem to understand. We have come to seize Lo Fan."

Kli Ning gasped in incredulity. Ai Char stepped in smoothly, "You see, Kli Ning, Clause 328 clearly apportions blame in such circumstances. I confess that I have been guilty of a slight clerical oversight. Lo Fan faces almost certain criminal charges for not safeguarding the use of his personal chop, under Article 7 of the Chopping Standards. Possibly death. It's difficult to say. I think the courts should determine this man's guilt and then sentence him, although not necessarily in that order."

Chih effused, "I am relieved to find that someone in this organisation appears to have a basic understanding of elementary public and criminal procedures. Clearly we must hold Lo Fan in custody, pending trial to confirm his evident guilt." With that, Chih motioned to the two police officers, who promptly seized Lo Fan. All four smartly marched from the room.

Kli Ning was furious and rounded on Ai Char. "Get a detailed grip on the big picture, Ai Char. You got us into this mess; you had better get Lo Fan out of it. And fast."

Ai Char unctuously declined. "I am a humble human remains... I mean human resources manager," he said, "handling legal proceedings is not in my job description. Handling legal proceedings is part of the general manager's job description. Lo Fan had better get moving on this very quickly, although as he is in jail I can see that this will be difficult. Perhaps you ought to find a new general manager who is capable of dealing with it. If you advertise the post, I would be happy to apply. Further, I think it is my duty to point out to you that you face almost certain civil proceedings to recover the funds you have misappropriated from the Seasonally Adjusted Transitional Employment Subsidy Scheme. That is, unless it is proved that the fraud was perpetrated by an employee acting outside the law."

Kli Ning was disgusted by Ai Char's lack of principles. Ai Char didn't even seem to be doing it for the money. Kli Ning was now totally confused between principles and money. Kli Ning therefore rushed off to see his lawyer, Mr Fat, known in the village as Fat Fee. After reviewing the documents and deliberating on Kli Ning's statements, Fat Fee commented, "Surely, Kli Ning, you knew that the Seasonally Adjusted Transitional Employment Subsidy Scheme was not meant to be used by businesses such as yours. Further, you know that the monthly submissions were a technical loophole. You were fortunate that Ai Char used Lo Fan's chop. Because we can now prove that the fraud was perpetrated by an employee acting outside the law, you can be sure to keep the subsidy money, less a small penalty fine. And naturally my fees."

Kli Ning seemed relieved, but enquired, "Yes, but what about Lo Fan?"

Fat Fee demurred, "You know how often I have had to advise you to get a detailed grip on the big picture. You are well aware that I am a commercial lawyer and not a criminal lawyer. Handling criminal proceedings is not in my job description. However, if you want my informal, unofficial, personal advice, if I were in your shoes I would dump the loser. I think Lo Fan will be unable to perform his duties for you for some years. Further, speaking as your friend, I would advise you to think twice before employing anyone with a criminal record."

Kli Ning was troubled. "What do you think will happen if I do intervene on Lo Fan's behalf? After all, this whole scheme was Ai Char's idea and not Lo Fan's. Unofficially, what do you advise?"

"For my friends, my unofficial fee rates are the same as my official ones, but never mind. If you do intervene on Lo Fan's behalf, you will almost certainly have to repay all the subsidy monies, plus a large penalty fine, plus of course my fees. If you give me a moment to calculate this on my personal abacus, that's, let's see, approximately nine months of your staff wages. Further, if you look at the documentation, any court would conclude from Ai Char's memo that Ai Char was clearly against this from the start and exercised considerable restraint on Lo Fan's excesses."

Kli Ning had a real problem. Two of his fundamental principles were in direct conflict: making money and looking after his people when they showed a good rate of return. He recalled the wise words of a man in whom, many years previously, Kli Ning had invested a great deal of money for a dreadful return; the late lamented knife sharpener who worked beside his first restaurant. "The people you help on your way up are slightly less likely to knife you on your way down." The knife sharpener finally proved his worth that day. Z/Yen enlightenment sometimes came from unlikely sources. Kli Ning now knew what he had to do.

A week later, Lo Fan was profoundly grateful and out of jail. Kli Ning and Lo Fan promptly implemented Lo Fan's original plan to make significant staff cuts by firing all senior staff. Over the next eighteen months, the savings were likely to cover the anticipated subsidy repayments and government fines. When Lo Fan submitted his list for senior staff dismissal, Kli Ning was not surprised to see Ai Char's name at the top of the list. Kli Ning happily signed the dismissal orders, pointedly using his own chop. Lo Fan settled back for a long, hard eighteen months. Lo Fan felt greatly indebted for all Kli Ning had done on his behalf, and resolved to pay Kli Ning back through his increased endeavours and enduring loyalty.

Some months and eighteen bureaucrats later, in the bowels of the town's brand new statistical annex, the earnest clerk, Min, was troubled. He had just received a Seasonally Adjusted Transitional Employment Subsidy Rebate and Penalty Fine form of such magnitude that, once implemented, would require nine months of work on statistical revisions for the prior two-year period. Inadvertently, Min mislaid all three copies of the Rebate and Penalty Fine

Form. This mishap saved Kli Ning a lot of money. Kli Ning never bothered to mention the savings to Lo Fan. Lo Fan was far too busy with his diligent work to notice the savings. Lo Fan did notice that a statistical clerk, Min, was the only civil servant he knew who ate at Kwik Klining Duck Tea Houses. Indeed, Min ate there every day. Min was also the only civil servant Lo Fan knew with a Lifetime Pass, which entitled him to a substantial discount on all food and drink purchases at any outlet of the Kwik Klining Duck Tea House and Laundry Franchise. Lo Fan pondered long and hard on the vicissitudes of life, before getting back to working off his debt to the ever-merciful Chao Kli Ning.

QUESTIONS FOR STUDENTS

Would you have bailed out Lo Fan or would you have let the loser stew? If your answer was to bail him out, determine the appropriate interest rate to charge, showing calculations where necessary.

Write an appropriate letter from Fat Fee, specifying the formal and informal advice to Chao Kli Ning, referencing appropriate case law where needed, and appending detailed fee calculations and disbursement of expenses, both incurred and wholly fictitious.

MOST PEOPLE ARE SHEEP. WHEN
OTHER PEOPLE'S ETHICS ARE THE
LAW, YOU MAY NOT HAVE ENOUGH
TIME TO DEAL WITH YOUR OWN

THE LAST WILL AND TESTAMENT OF CHAO KLI NING (CIRCA 400 BC)

I KNOW THAT HALF OF MY
MONASTERY DUES ARE WASTED,
THE PROBLEM IS THAT I DON'T
KNOW WHICH HALF

THE MOST LUCRATIVE THOUGHTS OF CHAO KLI NING
(FIFTY PER CENT LIKELIHOOD OF CORRECT ATTRIBUTION)

SAVING FAITH

When our protagonists invest heavily in dogma, reap the rewards of hard graft and discover the virtues of international pyramid sales.

LO FAN WAS HARDLY SURPRISED to hear Kli Ning complain about costs. Chao Kli Ning always complained about costs. To listen to Kli Ning, Lo Fan felt, was to believe that all the costs in the world were met from Kli Ning's pockets.

"O master, we must spend money on our monastery dues to the Brothers in Alms or our business will suffer," pleaded Lo Fan.

"Yes, Lo Fan, we must spend the money, but we should get more value for our money. At least half our money is wasted. And I say this as the former personal confessor of the Great Alm himself," replied Kli Ning.

"But, O master, if half our monastery dues are wasted, then surely we can find out which half is valuable and only spend that?" suggested Lo Fan. "Why are we wasting half our monastery dues?"

"Oh Lo Fan, you can be very trying. Get a big picture grip on the details. You've got to try to understand the complexities of PR (paying religion). These

monks understand the psyche of our target customers: passing pilgrims, fervent daily worshippers, doubters, agnostics, cynics and sceptical believers who hedge their bets. Our monks use sophisticated techniques to promote our products to our targets," explained Kli Ning.

"Like telling them to eat in our restaurant and wash in our laundry?" muttered Lo Fan. "Why can't we tell our customers ourselves?"

Kli Ning was visibly agitated, "Lo Fan, have you learned nothing from our years of association? There are a number of complex skills in dealing with pilgrims, worshippers and such like. For instance, there's, well, telling them about the um, um, restaurant and, um, laundry. As well as, um, telling them about the benefits of the, um, um, restaurant and, um, laundry. As you see, it's very complex and we couldn't possibly do it ourselves."

Sometimes Lo Fan had a persistent, almost childlike quality to his questions. "Kli Ning, don't the Sisters of Mo Tzi offer the same services?"

Now Kli Ning was upset, "Lo Fan, there is simply no way that the Sisters of Mo Tzi in their small convent could handle our sizeable account! You are well aware that the Sisters of Mo Tzi only handle jade accounts door-to-door. But, perhaps..." Kli Ning trailed off into thought.

A few days later, Kli Ning's neighbours couldn't help but notice the strange assortment of nine monastic orders trying to stay out of the sun. The monks and nuns sought shade along walls and under trees in Kli Ning's garden. Two particular monastic orders stood out from the crowd. In one corner of the garden, by the bo tree, the highly successful local order of nuns, the Sisters of Mo Tzi, were clearly practising some new evangelical chant accompanied by what appeared to be cheer-leading motions and explanatory flip-charts. Mo Tzi herself, the famed proponent of door-to-door proselytisation, seemed to create new chants for her order on the spot. In another corner, near the pagoda, the normally serene Brothers in Alms appeared positively sullen, muttering amongst themselves and passing around detailed analyses of the Kli Ning account gross billings and profitability.

The more curious of Kli Ning's neighbours hung about for a while, eager to share some of the Z/Yen enlightenment clearly about to occur in the vicinity of Kli Ning's house. If the locals had been any less eager to attain Z/Yen enlightenment, some less charitable gossips in the village might have said Kli Ning's neighbours were eavesdropping. The neighbours heard Lo Fan call each monastic order in turn. Several times the neighbours listened to a near identical speech by the head of the order, a series of totally identical questions from Kli Ning, the hastened departure of the order's delegation, sighs of relief from Kli Ning and earnest discussion between Kli Ning and Lo Fan.

As eavesdroppers, the neighbours were abject failures. They left the side of Kli Ning's house late in the afternoon thoroughly confused. These simple village folk were unable to assimilate straightforward religious concepts such as "the unique selling proposition", "positioning", "buyer purchase criteria", "brand extension" and "perpetual salvation that pays". All they could ascertain was that the Sisters of Mo Tzi had been permitted to chant for five minutes longer than anyone else and had generated the most earnest discussion between Kli

Ning and Lo Fan. The Sisters certainly were a most influential order, despite a well-known reliance on door-to-door jade accounts.

The very next day, each neighbour was surprised to be greeting one of the Sisters at their own front door. The Sisters explained that they had returned to the neighbourhood to extol the virtues of cleanliness, a healthy diet and value for money. The Sisters praised the Kli Ning laundry and restaurant for exemplifying these virtues. Pilgrims to the Sisters' convent were greeted by large signs glorifying the excellence of Kli Ning's establishments and its contribution to salvation. Lo Fan was amazed at how quickly attendance at the restaurant's luncheon sitting increased.

"Kli Ning, I'm amazed at how quickly the number of diners has increased this lunchtime," remarked Lo Fan.

"Ah well, Lo Fan, you see that this is the benefit of splitting our marketing budget between two religious establishments. Now we have both sides fighting for us. This division is something I have long recommended, as you are well aware."

The Brothers in Alms were up in arms about the Kli Ning account. Within a week, a delegation of belligerent Brothers descended on Kli Ning demanding the full account or nothing. The Brothers adamantly refused to share the Kli Ning account with a bunch of brazen women, led by the garish Mo Tzi, who insisted on using secular locations such as doorsteps to put their message across, rather than religious premises specifically designed for that purpose. The use of these secular locations could only lead to a decline in moral standards, an increasing crime rate, unwanted pregnancies and encouragement to encyclopaedia salesmen. The Brothers were emphatic that all of Kli Ning's PR should be done through one account. Kli Ning was happy to oblige. He explained to the Brothers that if it had to be only one account, then based on recent results, the Sisters had it. Most of the Brothers may have looked surprised at Kli Ning's decision, but the head of the order merely bowed his head sagely and explained to Kli Ning how joyful it must be to be so close to Z/Yen enlightenment. While the other Brothers listened in astonishment or, as the *Z/Yen Papers* later chronicled, rapture, the head of the order expressed his undying commitment to ecumenical work with the Sisters and proclaimed that Kli Ning had passed the head of the order's test of unselfishness.

Thus was it written that both orders would go forth to proclaim the message of Kli Ning's laundry and restaurant in harmony. The Brothers seemed to strive even harder after their awakening. Several of the Brothers appeared to bear the marks of religious education on their backs and legs after failing to make significant converts of passing pilgrims. Other Brothers seemed to drop their objections to using some of the Sisters' direct sales techniques, as long as it was for such a worthy cause.

Both orders seemed to have benefited from the healthy debate which Kli Ning had initiated. At least, that was what the heads of the Sisters and the Brothers said in prayer meetings. The Sisters attributed their new-found competitiveness directly to Kli Ning's account and had rapidly expanded outside just jade. In fact, the Sisters had recently won the Rice Express door-to-door delivery account while the Brothers had publicised their recent win of PR for the So Li Shirt Repair service.

Lo Fan was pleased to report a continuing rise in sales. Most of these new sales seemed to result from the passing pilgrim trade. Less satisfactorily, some of the regular customers had begun to seek other establishments where the whirr of prayer wheels played less havoc with digestion. Kli Ning could not be happier, but Lo Fan had to deal with some of the religious debates in the restaurant and at the laundry counter. The adherents of the Brothers in Alms could not abide some of the dietary fetishes of the followers of the Sisters of Mo Tzi. The acolytes of the Sisters could not countenance the garbs of the relatively unwashed devotees of the Brothers. The debates became altercations, the altercations became quarrels, the quarrels became brawls. The brawls were expensive and hurt business. Well, the brawls hurt Kli Ning's business. Rice Express and So Li Shirt Repair seemed to go from strength to strength. Sometimes passing pilgrims remarked that it was difficult to establish exactly for whom the Brothers and Sisters worked, but if you needed a cheap rice meal or a good shirt repair you knew where to go – and it wasn't Kli Ning's establishments.

Lo Fan was disappointed to report a continuing fall in sales to Kli Ning. As Lo Fan explained to a bemused Kli Ning, "Market research appears to evince a passing decline in correlated combined account purchases from separate PR campaigns whilst not undermining core purchase validity, although excessive religious affiliation could be a contributing consumer attribution."

"What are you trying to say, Lo Fan? Is this some religious jargon Mo Tzi has taught you?" asked Kli Ning.

"With the greatest and utmost respect, noble Sir, I believe that the Brothers' and Sisters' PR campaigns are hurting business," replied Lo Fan.

"Yes my loyal servant," agreed Kli Ning, "they stink. But what can we do? We need religious approval to attract the pilgrim trade. None of the towns-people want our food, because they seem to take hot meals delivered to their homes by Rice Express. None of the villagers want our laundry, because So Li handles it all. But still, we can't afford to stop paying the Brothers and Sisters. Sometimes, I just wish the fights would stop breaking out on our premises."

"Sir, I learned a new word when talking to a Beijing Mandarin yesterday. This word 'secular' is most confusing. Apparently it means something without religion, or a-religious or something. I am happy that I know of no restaurants or laundries so godless as to be secular. Isn't it frightening to have something so atheistic?" queried Lo Fan.

"Get a detailed grip on the big picture, my humble servant. Secular is hardly a frightening concept," assured Kli Ning. "In fact, as a well-travelled gentleman, I am familiar with many foreign lands where secular is not just known, but fervently believed," boasted Kli Ning.

"O learned master, how happy am I that these secular foreign concepts are banished from our lands so that we may experience the joys of intensive religious debate within our very premises, in order to enrich our daily lives and bring meaning to our otherwise worthless existence," observed Lo Fan.

Kli Ning pondered these platitudes for a moment and then burst forth.

"You are quite right Lo Fan, we shall celebrate the beauty of secularity. As I have always said, paying religion is a poor way to promote a business. If you can't do-it-yourself, don't ask a monk or nun. Let us be rid of both the Brothers in Alms and the Sisters of Mo Tzi. Let us be rid of this tithing mumbo-jumbo. Let us go forth the Z/Yen way, into the land of secularity where the rivers flow with business opportunities, the pavements are paved with paying customers and where prayer wheels never whirl."

Lo Fan may have been secretly pleased at Kli Ning's decision to go secular, but he never showed it. As sales rocketed under the new secular promotion (door-to-door sales, signs rented at nearby monasteries and a discrete blanket coverage leaflet campaign over several weeks which included a massive jackpot lottery), Kli Ning became more convinced of the efficacy of his do-it-yourself strategy. Unfortunately, as the secular promotion campaign grew, the task began to take up more and more of Lo Fan and Kli Ning's time. The pair began to realise the effort the Sisters and Brothers put into their marketing. In particular, Kli Ning began to resent frequent late-night interruptions, even at his exalted position, as they tried to rush out each last-minute campaign.

"Lo Fan," intoned Kli Ning, "I have begun a process that others may take up after me. And the sooner they take it up after me the better."

"O esteemed businessman," remarked Lo Fan, "only a fool would undertake something as risky as marketing from an internal position. Such a fool would be responsible for the marketing strategy and the hiring of a suitable sales force, and be held liable for any fall in sales. Besides, if this 'secular' stuff turns out to be invalid, the fool would be barred from salvation and Z/Yen enlightenment. Such a position would be a sure road to disaster."

"You are quite right Lo Fan," said Kli Ning. "I cannot fail to express every confidence in your abilities. May you create the most powerful sales force in the history of my restaurants and cleaning establishments. I, Kli Ning, give you the pyramid, a powerful symbol brought from far-off lands in the West. These western cultures are truly obsessed with sales and marketing. The pyramid is their most potent symbol, uniting the four forces of business beneath a focal point of stonemasonry. May you conquer many sales territories in its name. Thus have I spoken."

"You honour me above my humble abilities," demurred Lo Fan. "Much as I aspire to the role you have outlined, my other duties require me to maintain an impartiality in the religious disputes which appear to be making increasing interruptions to our formerly peaceful and lucrative trades. The role you describe in sales and marketing is profoundly religious, even if performed by a secular advocate such as myself."

Kli Ning frowned, pondered for a moment and replied, "Yes, now that you mention it, secular religious fervour is clearly beyond your capabilities. Sometimes I am slightly too hasty in my desire to resolve problems quickly and to promote loyal, albeit mediocre, staff. Yet we must seek a new organisation to undertake our marketing or continue to do it ourselves. Perhaps we could employ one of the Brothers or Sisters to enlist secular acolytes to perform our marketing? If only there were another agency to whom we could turn."

"O master, we began this pilgrimage in order to obtain value for money from our religious dues, half of which we believed we were wasting. Yet there seems to be no way to pay but half of our dues and still meet our targets," observed Lo Fan. "On reflection, perhaps there is another perspective on this problem. Half our dues to the Sisters of Mo Tzi go to Mo Tzi and half are wasted on the gaggle of other nuns who merely repeat the same chants. Curious, isn't it?"

On the following day, a press release was circulated throughout the province. The revered nun, Mo Tzi, had suddenly abandoned the order she had founded, taken up a secular position with a new agency, "Kli Ning Secular Promotional Communications" and adopted the pyramid as her symbol. Although Mo Tzi's work for Kli Ning is clearly documented historical fact, she and her agency achieved legendary status with their self-promotional efforts in pyramid selling and the power of pyramids.

Without denigrating her powers, even her most fervent admirers were surprised to see one of the most colossal, secular imperial deification campaigns undertaken by her agency supporting Mo Tzi's own ends so blatantly. Mo Tzi had promised some magnificent, nay outrageous, constructions in far-off lands to support the "pyramid campaign". Although some critics of Mo Tzi expressed surprise at the apparent rapidity of the construction, others admired the seemingly perfect patina of two and a half thousand years of age that Mo Tzi's set designers had given to the campaign's sets. Everyone admitted the exotic brilliance of her concept and even Mo Tzi's critics had to accept that the Imperial Audit Office had travelled to a distant western land, a region called "E-Gypt", and had assured itself that such vast sums had actually been spent in support of the campaign. Some of Mo Tzi's more persistent critics took pains to point out that the Imperial Audit Office should likewise have verified the more remote eastern portions of Mo Tzi's flamboyant campaign in "Amer Ika", where ludicrous sums had been expended clearing jungle for further erections of pyramids.

Mo Tzi's only comment on the enduring merit of the pyramid campaign was, "We built too many of the blasted pyramids in so many places. Half of these pyramids are wasted; the problem is that I don't know which half. Technology just always lets me down."

QUESTIONS FOR STUDENTS

Role play a door-to-door sales encounter first as a Sister of Mo Tzi and then as a Brother in Alms. Calculate the exact payback of each door opening.

Using papier mâché, encapsulate the entire PR strategy for Chao Kli Ning in a work of permanent sculpture suitable for exhibition and resale.

THE PEAK OF SUCCESS BEGINS IN THE FOUR CORNERS OF A FIRM FOUNDATION

FENG SHUI FOR FUN AND PROFIT

HOW CAN A WHOLE ORANGE TREE GROW
FROM A SEED IN BUT ONE SEGMENT?

(BELIEVED TO BE FROM) LO FAN'S DIARY

FAT CHANCE'S RISKY BUSINESS

Why has it taken so long for our characters to discover the basic theory of business? No matter, they have got there in the end.

"HOW TO MAKE SOME MORE MONEY? If only my business were as simple and clean as Fat Chance's," pondered Chao Kli Ning, famous restaurateur and laundry entrepreneur. He was thinking of his local racetrack bookie Mr Fat, known in the village as Fat Chance. Fat Chance seemed to have the simple business of cleaning out the villagers' wallets each time they went to the racetrack.

"Give Peace a chance," said Lo Fan, referring to Perpetual Peace, the strong favourite for the Village Cup. "Perpetual Peace may be the odds-on favourite, but his performance is such a dead certainty that you are bound to win some money despite the poor odds."

"Lo Fan, you can be truly trying," spat Kli Ning. "I was talking business. Perpetual Peace is a horse. Fat Chance's bookie operation is a business. I find it difficult to understand how Fat Chance can be so successful. How can he make money by playing games with the entire village? I must find out. I am sure

WHEN FAT CHANCE THE BOOKIE WAS LAYING
OFF BETS, WOE BETIDE A PASSING PUNTER
TRYING TO CROSS THE COURSE !

that his brother, the lawyer Fat Fee, has arranged some kind of legal angle to put the squeeze on honest gamblers."

"O noble master," began Lo Fan, seeing the onset of one of Kli Ning's irritable-soon-to-result-in-a-new-scheme-with-extra-work-for-Lo-Fan moods, "perhaps we could peruse the situation this weekend when I place my bet with Fat Chance."

Come the weekend, Lo Fan and Kli Ning made their respective excuses to their respective wives – pressures of work, need to investigate alternative business methods, the wives had to understand. The wives did understand, especially when they were asked to pack a picnic lunch. The wives wisely stayed mum; in any event, the longer the men were at the racetrack, the longer the wives had to entertain their friends and enjoy their own profitable enterprise, hosting a terracotta-ware party.

On the big day, Lo Fan had his heart set on getting to the bookie quickly. He knew the importance of placing bets early on a favourite. Lo Fan rapidly placed an each-way bet on the odds-on favourite, Perpetual Peace. Kli Ning should have noticed that Lo Fan's wager was rather significant for someone with such a restricted income, but that's another story.

Kli Ning was a bit more relaxed than Lo Fan. Although Kli Ning had kept it a bit of a secret, unlike most businessmen in the village, he had only a passing acquaintance with the racetrack. Kli Ning's had been a misspent youth: petty businesses, lucrative cash-based laundering, fly-by-night fast food stands, etc. Kli Ning never really had any time for the racetrack. Kli Ning's naivety was all too apparent when he went to place his first wager. Fat Chance was totally flummoxed by Kli Ning's insistence on an interest rate for his deposit. Fortunately, Lo Fan was close by to offer Kli Ning some paternal advice, "When the wind be in the East, put all your cash on Perpetual Peace."

Partially out of annoyance with Lo Fan's trite jingles, and partially out of annoyance with the complex jargon used for strange combinations of bets, Kli Ning placed some pocket money on a total outsider, War Wounded. When Fat Chance recovered his breath at the extravagant size of the sum, he managed to gasp and write out a betting slip, knowing that despite the perceived risk, this would be easy money as he could lay the risk off against the other bookies, as long as he moved quickly. And Fat Chance, despite his weight, could move quickly.

While Fat Chance raced around the course, laying off Kli Ning's extravagant wager, Kli Ning and Lo Fan sipped suitably alcoholic concoctions from their terracotta mugs. Perpetual Peace covered Lo Fan's stake by coming in second. Kli Ning's horse, War Wounded, came in several lengths ahead of the rest of the field (save Fat Chance, who had managed a faster pace on softer ground). Kli Ning could hardly conceal his lack of surprise. Lo Fan braced himself for impending irritation; Kli Ning was benefiting from beginner's luck and would be positively unbearable about War Wounded's win.

Lo Fan and Kli Ning fell out over the next race. Nodding Nag and Speedy Stallion were favourite and outsider, respectively, although some found this difficult to guess from their names. Ai Char, one of the village's experts on trivia and part of the increasing band of former Kli Ning employees, had no problems guessing that the names of the horses were inversely related to their likely positions. Ai Char studied the form.

"Ai Char, long time, no see," said Kli Ning, interrupting Ai Char's concentration. "All's well on the job front, I trust," observed Kli Ning, with his typical aplomb and delicacy in small talk. "What's that bunch of numbers you're studying?"

"Ah, well I wouldn't expect of man of rash judgements such as yourself to invest time in proper decision making, but this is the racing form," answered Ai Char caustically. "Chance favours only the prepared, and I am prepared. I use this information carefully to select horses whose odds are not commensurate with their past performance and, I hope, their potential."

"Get a big picture grip on the details, Ai Char. It seems like a lot of effort for a bit of fun. Besides, I don't study the form, and I always seem to get it right," rebuked Kli Ning as he extrapolated wildly from his sole lifetime wager.

"Well, all I can say is that you either 'bribe the gods' or bet once in a lifetime," replied Ai Char, both enviously and suspiciously close to the mark. "Anyway, I have to go. Time's closing for this race and I need to get my cash on True-2-Form."

"What about Nodding Nag and Speedy Stallion?" asked Kli Ning. "Surely, your wager is better placed on a certainty or a high pay-out?"

"Well, as you are so unprepared, you won't have noticed True-2-Form's consistent improvement against comparable fields; excellent odds given the risk," pontificated Ai Char. "Anyway, I have to run. I trust you've managed to stay in business of late," he called out over his shoulder.

Lo Fan sped by Kli Ning on his way to lay a bet on the favourite, Nodding Nag. Kli Ning raced off after Lo Fan to place his bet on the outsider, Speedy Stallion. Again, because of the size of Kli Ning's wager, Fat Chance began an exercise routine that made the horses look as if they were merely greyhounds circling a course without a hare.

When the results of the race came in, Lo Fan and Kli Ning had already moved several inches down the bar drinks menu. In the end, Lo Fan was vindicated. Nodding Nag had comfortably seen off Speedy Stallion and Lo Fan had established a convincing two-inch lead over Kli Ning on the alcoholic menu. Unfortunately, Nodding Nag had not seen off any other contenders and Lo Fan was well on his way to the mother-of-all-hangovers. Lo Fan and Kli Ning lost their stakes, utterly, completely and totally. One more such "victory" over Kli Ning and Lo Fan would be undone.[8] Kli Ning began a spirited argument with Lo Fan, which began by questioning Lo Fan's irresponsibility in poorly advising an innocent, novice gambler. Kli Ning went on to question Lo Fan's suitability for managerial business positions given his poor luck. Kli Ning ended his argument by questioning the virtue of certain of Lo Fan's family members. Lo Fan retaliated with some choice comments, but was saved from irreparable outbursts by Ai Char's interruption.

---

[8]   Lo Fan might have called it a Pyrrhic victory, but for the fact that Pyrrhus would not be born for another 150 years and, even then, at some distance from the village racetrack.

"Although I hate to intrude on such lovingly-crafted base insults," interjected Ai Char, "I'm sure that both of you noticed the importance of superiority of form. Even more importantly, as my horse True-2-Form came in second, I'm sure that both of you noticed the importance of balancing odds against potential performance. I'm sure that you've learned something today, although these things can take time to sink in with certain types. Anyway, have to rush. See you next time, losers."

Kli Ning and Lo Fan had learned something. Thanks to Ai Char, their fight could wait till another day. Sadly for Lo Fan, Kli Ning had the inklings of learning something – business also seemed to be all about risk and reward. Fat Chance knew something else that the business duo had little chance of learning quickly – business might well be all about risk and reward, but the only way to make real money was to dominate the betting system (although total domination seemed to involve significant amounts of exercise).

"There is nothing special about my business, Lo Fan," elucidated Kli Ning the following day in the office. "This is just like the racetrack. We place some bets based on our interpretation of the form. If we work them well, we win – big time!" Fat Chance may have had a richer description of the complexity of events surrounding bets, but Kli Ning had clearly grasped the essence of the previous day's activities.

"Well try this problem then," interjected Lo Fan. "I have two business proposals from two of your employees before me. Bli Ching tells me that we must move into hospital bedding for the laundry. Sik Chao is adamant that the hospitals will buy our food long before we can sell them laundry services. Which proposal should I choose? Or both? Or neither? How will your current infatuation with speculation illuminate us?"

Kli Ning offered Lo Fan some paternal advice. "You have to speculate to accumulate! To your problem then, Lo Fan. You must ask Bli Ching and Sik Chao what is the balance of risk and reward for their proposals. I suggest that you allocate two-thirds of our enterprise funding to the best proposal and one-third to the second best."

Bli Ching made a stunning case to Lo Fan for the benefit to the Kwik Klining Duck Tea House and Laundry of hospital laundry services. Her exposition became a bit technical, while slogans, such as "whiter than white", seemed to fall off her tongue. Bli Ching had studied the market, the requisite supporting operations, the pricing, the promotion and the packaging. She concluded with a convincing punchline: "Hospital laundry can remove blood, sweat and cash from tight-fisted hospital administrators worldwide." Lo Fan saw the extensive merits of pursuing hospital laundry, although he fervently hoped that the blood would wash off the cash.

Sik Chao developed an entrancing story. People eat. People get sick. People go to hospital. People eat food in hospital. People get well or die. Dead people don't eat. Cured people continue to eat the food they ate in hospital in order to stay alive. The logic was inescapable. If the Kwik Klining Duck Tea House fed people in hospital, not only would the Kwik Klining Duck Tea House make money catering to hospitals, but the business would have customers for life – or at least until the customers visited a hospital for the last time (and even funerals need catering, thought Lo Fan, always anxious to develop a lively idea). Sik Chao finished with a flourish, "Remember, hospital food is for life customers, not just for sick people; and a Kli Ning Chao meal a day keeps the doctor away."

Lo Fan exited before Sik Chao could elaborate on some of his other marketing ideas, such as further health slogans relating anatomical parts to various animals, fruits and vegetables. Lo Fan needed to think on Kli Ning's remonstration, what was the balance of risk and reward. Lo Fan was captivated by Sik Chao's proposal. The risks were high, e.g. headlines such as "Food Poisoning Kills the Terminally Ill." The rewards were high. Sik Chao's forecasts were phenomenal. Lo Fan's sensible nature gave him natural sympathies for Bli Ching's straightforward low-risk, moderate-reward proposal.

Lo Fan set things in motion. He also returned to inform Kli Ning. "O master, on the balance of risk and reward, Sik Chao was measured and found wanting. I have chosen the sensible risk and reward of Bli Ching for the majority of the enterprise funding."

"Lo Fan, get a detailed grip of the big picture," expounded Kli Ning. "In the portfolio of life, a balance must always be struck. Choosing Bli Ching's proposal gives us another low-risk, low-reward project. Yet how can we ever achieve the high gains that Fat Chance obtains if we weight our portfolio with low-risk, low-reward activities? Where is the opportunity to make a quick buck? What have I wrought with my infatuation with speculation?" Kli Ning nervously fiddled with his new worry beads – strange six sided cubes blessed by a lucky monk, with subtle arrangements of dots on each side. Lo Fan slunk away, leaving Kli Ning deep in thought.

As is more than usual with committed senior managers such as Lo Fan and Kli Ning, they were both far too busy dealing with complex risk/reward analysis to spend much time on the sales front with Sik Chao and Bli Ching. Sik Chao was finding it hard going. Hospitals did need good food, but they wanted a trial period and trial periods cost money. With only one-third the budget he required, Sik Chao would need a very long time to develop the hospital food market. Bli Ching was also finding it hard going. True, the funding she required was in place, but for some reason the hospitals had too few tough stains to clean. Without tough stains, hospitals would only pay a minimal price for laundry cleaning. And funerary shrouds seemed to get buried.

One fine day, Bli Ching secretly went to visit one of Sik Chao's client hospitals. She bumped into a former colleague, Ai Char, who was languishing in traction in a bed. Apparently Ai Char had been injured while gambling at the racetrack. He had made the near-fatal mistake of crossing the racetrack in front of a heavy, fast-moving herd, led by a particularly single-minded beast. When Fat Chance the bookie was laying off bets, woe betide a passing punter trying to cross the course. The doctors agreed that all four limbs broken in one incident was rare and unlucky, but Ai Char would probably be out of hospital in a mere six weeks.

"You look great Ai Char," said Bli Ching, addressing Ai Char's tractioned, bandaged foot, momentarily mistaking it for Ai Char's tractioned, bandaged head.

"Hmm," replied Ai Char.

"You do really look great," said Bli Ching, re-orienting herself to Ai Char's head. "However, this bed is a real mess. Look at this; there's food everywhere. And all these stains. These sheets could be whiter than white if only I had the laundry contract for this hospital. In fact, if I had a contract for each hospital that Sik Chao serves, with all the food he's doling out and all the food stains that implies, what a business. Sik Chao's menu could easily feature staining curries, unremovable egg and even beetroot. Just think of the stains. With all those sales commissions, Sik Chao and I could both spend much more time with Fat Chance at the racetrack."

At this point, Ai Char appeared to go apoplectic. Bli Ching was surprised that Ai Char was so supportive, particularly where Fat Chance was concerned, but Ai Char was well known for studying the form better than most.

As will be apparent to even the most casual reader, Sik Chao and Bli Ching teamed up to form an insuperable partnership. Sik Chao's staining recipes combined with Bli Ching's stain-removal formulae were able to produce outrageous revenues for the Kwik Klining Duck Tea House and Laundry. Yet, not so outrageous profits, and, like Lo Fan, for several years, Sik Chao and Bli Ching made outrageous claims for expenses and appeared to place wagers with Fat Chance which were rather significant for Kli Ning employees on such restricted incomes.

Soon after the combined enterprise took off, Kli Ning and Lo Fan visited Ai Char in hospital. Kli Ning and Lo Fan were not the sort of bosses to ignore a former employee when he was down on his luck, not even a nit-picking troublemaker like Ai Char, especially at a time when Kli Ning and Lo Fan themselves were doing so well and would be able to cheer up the wretched Ai Char with news of his former employer's soaring revenues in the hospital catering and laundry markets.

At Ai Char's bedside, following a mere fifteen-minute exposition by Kli Ning espousing his new risk/reward technique for investment appraisal and the resulting inevitability of success, Lo Fan finally chipped in, "Yes, but despite the detailed analysis we undertook, the result was a complete reversal of our expectations. We thought that the laundry element would yield the lion's share of growth and gain, whereas in reality it is the food element of the enterprise which has proved to be the real 'rising starfish'. True, the laundry business which results from the food sales is a 'fat cow', but without that combination of the two services, hospital laundry would be a 'dead dog'.[9] It was like going to Fat Chance and winning money on the favourite and the outsider in the same race. Boy, did we get lucky."

"Hmm," remarked Ai Char, apoplectic with apparent joy and support for Lo Fan's statements, especially the analogy with Fat Chance and the racetrack.

Kli Ning, however, did not seem so pleased. "Much as I hate to bicker with you, Lo Fan, especially in front of a miserable, unfortunate former employee

---

[9] In Hunan province, it has been common practice for businessmen throughout the millennia to describe the success of business opportunities in terms of their favourite dishes on the restaurant menu.

such as Ai Char, I disagree wholeheartedly with your analysis of our success. Firstly, your constant reference to the racetrack is irritating beyond belief. Betting through Fat Chance is a mug's game; the only person who is making real money at the racetrack is Fat Chance. You should try your luck at my other new venture, the Kwik Klining Duck, Tea, Laundry and Craps Emporium. Dice are the only sensible way to wager; they are relatively clean and safe, and I run all the dice games in this province. But that's not important right now. More to the point, our success with hospital food and laundry was not down to luck at all. It was an excellent case study in total portfolio management. I am astonished that neither of you has grasped the essence of risk and reward. As my business grows I can take larger risks for larger rewards on individual projects, just as Fat Chance can take high-odds bets from the entire village as long as he has a large portfolio. Despite the size, extent and diversity of my business empire, indeed, partly because of those characteristics, my business is actually as simple as Fat Chance's. All businesses are gambling portfolios. This is the essence of Z/Yen."

At this point in the ancient text, sadly, the scrolls have become faded and damaged. Many scholars have tried unsuccessfully to reconstruct the conclusion of this tale. It is clear that Ai Char became apoplectic again at this juncture, to such a degree that medical intervention was required. The extent to which Ai Char recovered from this fit, if at all, is now lost in the mists of time, although he is clearly absent from later scrolls. More tragically, Kli Ning's ultimate exposition on the simplicity of risk/reward and total portfolio management, if indeed such an ultimate exposition ever existed, has gone forever. This loss has been much to the benefit of countless generations of professional advisors, but much to the detriment of countless generations of businessmen since Kli Ning's time.

■ Explain the tax benefits of using racehorses as part of your off-balance sheet investment programme. State the appropriate criminal sentences, or required bribes, if caught, for one, five and ten racehorses.

■ Recalculate the Kwik Klining Duck Tea House and Laundry's accounts using risk/reward probability distribution functions and real option theory.

■ Bonus question: explain the benefits of the trifecta and its similarity to the capital asset pricing model.

GIVEN THE CHOICE BETWEEN
SKILFUL RISK/REWARD MANAGERS
AND LUCKY RISK/REWARD MANAGERS,
I WOULD CHOOSE LUCKY RISK/REWARD
MANAGERS EVERY TIME

CHAO'S LITTLE RED BOOK ON SEARCH AND SELECTION

WHEN YOU KNOW YOU'RE GONNA GO,
YOU GOTTA BLOW YOUR DOUGH

LAST WILL AND TESTAMENT OF CHAO KLI NING
(UNEARTHED IN ITALY TOGETHER WITH SOME UNUSUALLY
SHAPED NOODLES, PROBABLY A 15TH CENTURY FORGERY)

SEE YOU, Z/YEN

How a magnificent business philosophy was established due to the munificence of a great man – and further funding from his children's, and his children's children's gambling debts.

"ALL GOOD THINGS MUST COME TO AN END," said Chao Kli Ning, the venerable businessman of his village, region and country as he left the gaming table. A shrill chorus of children's screams greeted his remark – "You can't leave now, Grandpa! How can you? You always leave when we've run out of money! Why can't we ever use your pair of lucky dice?"

Kli Ning seemed oblivious to their protests, patting each grandchild on the head, and collecting IOUs from some of the more impoverished, inveterate losers. Kli Ning walked towards his mansion, past the still thriving, original business which had made him a household name in these parts, the Kwik Klining Duck Tea House and Laundry. As he walked, he mused on enforcing some of the IOUs by leaning on his own children for their offspring's debts, purely in the interest of teaching his progeny not to participate in a rigged game. However, his thoughts soon moved from familial extortion to his forthcoming weekly tea with his loyal retainer and general manager, Lo Fan.

Lo Fan hurried his step as he bustled towards Kli Ning's mansion. Lo Fan knew Kli Ning would probably be a bit late; collecting from his grandchildren always took a bit of time. On this particular occasion, Lo Fan was especially keen to resolve an outstanding personal issue – his elevation to esteemed executive elder status, with all of the additional benefits that status implied: a regular stipend, tax-advantageous "business trips", occasional consultancy fees plus virtually unlimited free time to spend with his grandchildren and goldfish. For Lo Fan, today's meeting with Kli Ning would seal the rewards of a lifetime's dedication to the highest standards of fast food and textile maintenance services.

After the ceremonies of tea and the usual update on business, Lo Fan carefully chose the moment to broach the subject of his esteemed executive elder status. "O esteemed master," began Lo Fan, hoping that a sycophantic start would lead to a sympathetic solution, "we have worked long and hard together for many a year and my auspicious anniversary of birth is fast approaching. We have spoken several times before about the transition in my role which should be the natural consequence of my seniority."

"Ah," said Kli Ning, "you are speaking of your retirement. I suppose it is natural for a man of your age and limited ability to wish to leave the rather unrewarding affairs of business behind, in search of the joys of sitting at home with your family. I suppose it is fortuitous for our business that I have already spent such great efforts on preparing your assistant, Hai Fan, for high office. I feel that he will be a worthy successor to you."

"Oh esteemed and far-sighted master," riposted Lo Fan, hoping that a syco-phantic riposte would prevent a disadvantageous resolution, "given our previous discussions, my lifetime of devoted service and the penury of my personal savings, I had rather hoped for esteemed executive elder status based on my potential future contributions to the business. As you know, many of my past contributions were wrapped up in my pension plan, much of which we misapplied in that ill-fated investment fund for advanced cleaning automata."

"All's well that ends well," explained Kli Ning insensitively. "That's the way the fortune cookie crumbles – to coin a phrase. Anyway, I'm sure that the paucity of your personal finance hardly precludes some comfortable twilight years. Despite your investments in advanced cleaning automata, you know that our business is unable to recompense your losses and, even if we were to consider compensating you, the tax effect would be prohibitive. Besides, esteemed executive elder status is reserved for the select few who deserve significant post-employment compensations and benefits in order to secure the application of their wisdom for future business endeavours. Get a big picture grip on the details. I hardly think that a mere forty years with the Kwik Klining Duck Tea House and Laundry qualifies you as a repository of significant wisdom. This may seem harsh, but I mean my remarks as an informative appraisal."

"Oh esteemed, far-sighted and tax-efficient master," opined Lo Fan, hoping that a sycophantic phrase would avert an impecunious disaster, "whilst I admire, and indeed would normally support, your caring appraisal of the risk/reward potential of my future, the only asset I have to sell in my twilight years is the wisdom I have gained from involvement with your enterprises under your tutelage. It would seem a shame for me to have to top up my denuded pension with consultancy income derived from work for competing restaurants and laundries as well as occasional paid assistance to tax investigating authorities seeking business insights. As you are well aware, many businessmen protect their key employees' knowledge by paying slightly more over the years against an exclusivity agreement. You, very wisely, perceived that loyalty did not need payment, as long as the restaurant and laundry skills were transferred from the older employees to the newer employees. It is a shame that, of the newer employees, so many of the skills are vested in one individual, Hai Fan."

"Lo Fan," interrupted Kli Ning, "despite your limitations, perhaps wisdom is of some importance in business. On reflection, it is only right and proper that a long-serving individual such as yourself, a font of knowledge of our operations, should retain an esteemed position as the principal source of training for the newer employees of the Kwik Klining Duck Tea House and Laundry."

"Oh esteemed, far-sighted, tax-efficient and insightful master," observed Lo Fan, hoping that a sycophantic observation might multiply his tenuous gains, "surely a mere training course could not possibly reflect on the wisdom I have to transmit – a wisdom not born from my humble experiences, but gained from years of exposure to you in action. Training would hardly do your wisdom justice. A temple is the only establishment worthy of custody for such wisdom. Your name should be enshrined as founder of the first institution dedicated to the wisdom of business affairs. Monks of Business Affairs would go forth to spread your teachings to the far corners of the earth, naturally with exclusivity clauses preventing them from sharing their wisdom with fast food and laundry establishments."

"Lo Fan, you are right to recognise your limited absorption of my teachings. Yet from your abject position, you are also right to recognise that to call this wisdom *training* is demeaning. Running a Kwik Klining Duck Tea House and Laundry is not just a profession, it is a philosophy of life. In fact, it is not just a philosophy of life, it is a way of life. It does deserve a temple. There ought to be a monastery dedicated to preserving and teaching this way of life. If only the monks could see the importance of my teachings and some of the tax-efficient ways in which the donations could be combined with our business."

"Oh esteemed, far-sighted, tax-efficient, insightful and ever-enterprising master", complimented Lo Fan, hoping that a sycophantic egging-on might build an even more favourable result, "such narrow-mindedness is typical of the monastic orders. They are so obsessed with religion that they often lose sight of the substantial financial rewards here on earth. If they can't dress their teachings up in some mumbo-jumbo, some marketing mystique, they are rarely interested in true enlightenment."

"Ah, enlightenment in business," mused Kli Ning. "Now there's a concept. I bet that would sell. If only we had a snazzy, thrilling name for our business philosophy, something like Improved Business Performance or Totally Total Re-engineering. No, perhaps it should be short and snappy, say Yen, like the Yen Buddhists. You could even be the chief Yen monk, training my acolytes."

"Well, Yen is good and implies a craving. As we know, the only great sales opportunities are philosophies or dependencies or drugs," observed Lo Fan, realising that sycophantic preambles were unnecessary as he approached the winning straight, "but there are already Yen philosophies, Yen money, Yen restaurants, the yin-yang lot and even Yen – the Cantonese Craving (opium). Perhaps we should look for something more philosophical and exotic sounding, say Zen?"

"Zen sounds philosophical and implies enlightenment," cogitated Kli Ning. "But speaking as a professional marketeer, Zen is a great name for a philosophy but a terrible name for a religion. Get a detailed grip on the big picture. It would never catch on with the monks. Without a catchy name, a monastic institution is bound to fail. Perhaps we won't need the services of a chief monk after all."

"Oh esteemed, far-sighted, tax-efficient, insightful, ever-enterprising and sensitive master," murmured Lo Fan, hoping that a lengthy sycophantic phrase might buy him some thinking time. "Why not combine the philosophy of enlightenment with the craving for money. Zen is a good philosophy word; Yen is a good desire word. Combine the two. Let's call your wonderful Total Business Philosophy and Way of Life, Zen/Yen or Z/Yen – a philosophical desire to make money. Business people would pay a fortune for a well packaged philosophy."

Kli Ning was ecstatic. After a few weeks of arguing with his children's and grandchildren's lawyers, plus some subtle pressure regarding gambling debts, he was able to convince the more militant of his family that an educational foundation would prove to be the best way of passing on his inheritance. Lo Fan gained great prestige as the chief monk of Z/Yen. As the chief chronicler of Chao Kli Ning's teachings, Lo Fan presided over many Chao family conflicts in the years after the great man's death. In making his difficult judgements as executor of Kli Ning's estate, Lo Fan used fully his position as head of the most pre-eminent religious business order in the region, as well as a set of lucky dice which Kli Ning had mysteriously left to him. Lo Fan's impartiality in judgement was legendary, especially when a key decision required one of six choices. As he remarked himself, judgement fees with substantial book rights ensured him a seriously comfortable lifestyle.

In the centuries that followed Kli Ning and Lo Fan, the school of Z/Yen flourished under the skilful direction of Lo Fan's successors, wielders of Kli Ning's original Z/Yen chop.

$$\overline{Y}en$$

Disciples dispersed to the many corners of the soon-to-be-round earth. Many disciples' businesses flourished too. Where the disciples' businesses did not flourish, the disciples retrained as Monks of Business Affairs and turned to teaching the business of Z/Yen. And thus were many pointless and repetitive business books born. Thankfully, the passing of the ages, and some darn good bonfires at business libraries, have saved scholars the trouble of translating most of the obscure works, although many of the original "Totally Total" concepts can still be found in *The Z/Yen Papers* – the extant manuscript remnants of Chao Kli Ning, restaurateur, launderer and man with an uncanny knack for spotting an opportunity to make a quick buck.

QUESTIONS FOR STUDENTS

Devise a test to calibrate the fairness or unfairness skew of Chao Kli Ning's lucky dice. Warning: these dice might be heavily loaded, so do use appropriate safety equipment.

Draft a will for Chao Kli Ning which protects Z/Yen's intellectual property rights for the benefit of Kli Ning's immediate descendants and those of Lo Fan in perpetuity. Ensure that the will contains sufficient loopholes to provide you with substantial, personal risky rewards the Z/Yen way.

THE DEVIL IS NOT IN THE DETAIL,
THE DEVIL IS NOT EVEN IN THE BIG
PICTURE. GET A GRIP, THE DEVIL
IS A GREAT MARKETING DEVICE
(LOOSELY TRANSLATED) FROM THE BEST-SELLING
ORTHODOX TENETS OF CHAO KLI NING